Russians in the *Waffen-SS*

Russians in the *Waffen-SS*

29. Waffen-Grenadier-Division der SS "RONA" (russische Nr. 1)

30. Waffen-Grenadier-Division der SS (russische Nr. 2)

SS-Verband "Drushina"

Rolf Michaelis

Schiffer Military History
Atglen, PA

Book Translation by David Johnston

Book Design by Stephanie Daugherty.

Library of Congress Control Number: 2009929043

Printed in China.
ISBN: 978-0-7643-3348-4

This book was originally published in German under the title
Russen in der Waffen-SS
29. Waffen-Grenadier-Division der SS "RONA" (russische Nr.1)
30. Waffen-Grenasier-Division der SS (russische Nr.2)
SS-Verband "Drushina"

We are interested in hearing from authors with book ideas on related topics.

Published by Schiffer Publishing Ltd.
4880 Lower Valley Road
Atglen, PA 19310
Phone: (610) 593-1777
FAX: (610) 593-2002
E-mail: Info@schifferbooks.com.
Visit our web site at: www.schifferbooks.com
Please write for a free catalog.
This book may be purchased from the publisher.
Please include $5.00 postage.
Try your bookstore first.

In Europe, Schiffer books are distributed by:
Bushwood Books
6 Marksbury Avenue
Kew Gardens
Surrey TW9 4JF, England
Phone: 44 (0) 20 8392-8585
FAX: 44 (0) 20 8392-9876
E-mail: Info@bushwoodbooks.co.uk.
Visit our website at: www.bushwoodbooks.co.uk

Table of Contents

Foreword

Prior to the outbreak of war in 1941, the Soviet Union comprised approximately 170 million people of various nationalities. The Russian people formed the largest group, followed by the Ukrainians.

During the war almost one-million Soviet citizens sided with the Germans more or less willingly. Of these, approximately 15,000 Russians served in the *Waffen-SS*.

The purpose of this book is to document a segment of German and European military history that has been almost totally ignored by writers and researchers.

The book is based not just on files in the federal archives in Berlin, Freiburg, and Coblenz, but also on the memories and documents of former members and German soldiers who are in contact with these Russian volunteers. My thanks to all of them for their help and support.

This book is presented to the public in the hope that it will shed light on another chapter of history.

Berlin, October 2002
Rolf Michaelis

Introduction

"I will never need an order from the Führer to form new divisions, rather I will constantly gather personnel and arm them as soon as we have weapons and equipment, so that one day I can ask the Führer: My Führer, where can you use a division? For that is how I view the job of commander of the Replacement Army."

Thus declared *Reichsführer-SS* Himmler on 3 August 1944 at a meeting of Gauleiters in Posen. This followed his appointment as commander of the Replacement Army after the attempt on Hitler's life on 20 July 1944.

Just four days earlier, during a visit to the *Wolfsschanze*, the *Führer*'s East Prussian headquarters, he had turned this desire into fact by ordering the formation of the 29th and 30th Waffen-Grenadier-Divisions of the SS (Russian[1] Numbers 1 and 2).

In view of his earlier racial ideology, Himmler's formation of Russian units within the *Waffen-SS* was an absolute paradox, and demonstrated clearly the situation in which the German command found itself.

This book will now document the story of these two foreign units of the *Waffen-SS* and show what value they were to Germany.

The 29th Waffen-Grenadier-Division of the SS "RONA" (Russian No. 1)

The People's Defense Brigade "Rona"[2]

Formation and Combat in the Self-Governed District of Lokot

The history of "RONA," or the Russian People's Liberation Army, began quite unspectacularly. As in all the *rayons*[3] conquered by the German Armed Services after the start of the Eastern Campaign on 22 June 1941, they also installed a non-Communist mayor in Lokot (south of Briansk).

Ivan Voskoboynik,[4] who assumed the position in autumn 1941, differed from most of the other indigenous mayors, however, in that he and his deputy Bronislav Kaminski[5] also became politically active. On 25 November 1941 they formed the National-Socialist Russian Workers Party. Because of Germany's *Ostpolitik* and its disinterest in such activities in principal, however, the new party got no farther than a first manifesto.

In the hope of at least participating in the political organization of Russia following a German victory of arms, Voskoboynik and Kaminski abandoned political agitation by their party and instead became active in the military sphere.

This chapter of Russian collaboration, which was soon to become quite extraordinary, also had innocuous beginnings. Voskoboynik formed an order service, first with 20 and then 50 men, to maintain order in the villages of the *rayon*. Soon, however, it was also fighting the Soviet partisans who were appearing in ever growing numbers.

Without German knowledge, the mayor added former Red Army men and civilians, all volunteers, enlarging the order service into a combat force several hundred men strong. For about eight weeks, unknown to the Germans, the unit operated against the Soviet partisans in the huge wooded area around Lokot. Its weapons and equipment had been collected from stocks abandoned by the Red Army in the surrounding forests—the same source used by the majority of Soviet partisans.

Voskoboynik died on 8 January 1941. The official account stated that he had died in a partisan ambush[6]; however, there was some evidence to suggest that Kaminski had had him assassinated in order to seize power himself. A former member recalled:

"At the time a rumor quickly spread among us that Kaminski had been responsible for the ambush. From then on Voskoboynik's widow—a very stylish woman—worked as Kaminski's

secretary and later even for Major-General Bunyatshenko[7] *in the 600th Infantry Division (Russian).*

It is also interesting that Voskoboynik's brother Jüri joined us in 1942. He had been captured by the Germans as a captain and commander of a Soviet pioneer battalion, and an aggressive search by his sister-in-law located him in a prisoner of war camp. He came to Lokot, where he became commander of our pioneer battalion, which in fact was no more than a reinforced company. A structural and civil engineer by trade, he went to the 600th Infantry Division where he became a major and took over its pioneer battalion. He was killed in the fighting in Prague in 1945."

Headquarters, 2nd Army became aware of the anti-Communist combat unit in mid-January 1942 following a chance encounter between German railway construction workers and members of the Lokot People's Defense in the forests south of Briansk. *Generalleutnant* Bernhard,[8] the commander responsible for securing the hinterland, displayed much more farsightedness than many other German generals and took a favorable view of Kaminski, now the mayor, and his independent actions. After a meeting with *Generalleutnant* Bernhard, on 1 March 1942 Kaminski announced to the citizens of the *rayon* of Lokot:

"At the meeting with the general staff of the German Armed Services, General Brand [correctly: Bernhard] expressed his gratitude to me and the entire administration of our district for our good work.

As an expression of this gratitude, the Wehrmacht [general] has ordered that all employees of the rayon, the police and the commanders be given pieces of land and horses.

As well, the rayons of Susemka and Navlya have been transferred to us.

This order is being brought to the attention of the entire population of the district and I am convinced that in the future we will work together with the friendly German people, for the blossoming and prosperity of the great Russian people and our beloved Fatherland."

Generalleutnant Bernhard had thus fulfilled a long-held wish by the Russian farmers for an end to collective agriculture and a piece of land of their own. To him—named commander of Rear Army Area 352 on 1 April 1942—the Russian volunteers represented a welcome reinforcement in the struggle against the Soviet partisans. In addition to German security battalions and the Royal Hungarian 102nd and 108th Light Divisions, Bernhard now had under his command the Lokot People's Defense, which had grown to approximately 1,400 men.

At that time Kaminski was already calling his unit "the first national Russian army":

"All the battalions of the rayon of Lokot are joining (…) behind the combined leadership of the commander of the armed forces of the district of Lokot, Mr. Mironenko, and the chief of staff Mr. Balachov, to carry out an independent combat operation in the rayons of Susein and Komaritschi. Am firmly convinced that the first national Russian army will strike a destructive blow against the common enemy of the Russian people. Forward for a bright happy life!"

The fighting that subsequently developed in the Komaritschi area between 3 and 11 March 1942 was the fiercest to date. The People's Defense, most of whom were clad in Red Army uniforms, engaged about 2,000 partisans.

A representative of the Foreign Office attached to Headquarters, 2nd Army noted of Kaminski and the People's Defense in April 1942:

"Kaminski could definitely be used as a propagandist for a German new order in the east, provided certain aspects of the Russian mentality are taken into account. As well, experience in the military field shows that we will never be able to pacify the rear areas without Russian militia units familiar with the area and terrain. The units of our allies are not up to this task, quantitatively or qualitatively. On the contrary, as it has unfortunately turned out, the behavior of the Hungarian units in particular has caused rising resentment among the population [...] The employment of units, like Kaminski's for example, in the military circle pushes men with political leadership skills over into the military obedience system. In this way it will be easier to guide these men and their groups than by leaving them to their own devices or suddenly banning them."

While Army Group Center's front area became quieter after mid-April 1942, in the area of *Korück 532* (*Korück* = commander rear army area) problems were growing with Soviet partisan units—which since the winter of 1942-43 had been formed themselves from Red Army stragglers. In response to this threat, in May 1942 the 4th Army north of Briansk and the 2nd Panzer Army south of Briansk launched a pincer attack against the partisans. To head the operation, Headquarters, 2nd Panzer Army selected the commander of the 216th Infantry Division, *Generalleutnant* Freiherr von und zu Gilas[9], whose division was scattered over various sectors of the front. Gilsa was to engage the estimated 15,000 to 20,000 partisans in the Lokot area (75 km south of Briansk) to the Desna River in an area about 30 kilometers wide. To accomplish this task the general formed the "von Gilsa" Group with approximately 15,000 men:

Division headquarters with squad of military police
Signals Battalion 216
3rd Company/Pioneer Battalion 216
Infantry Regiment 348
Heavy IV Battalion/Artillery Regiment 216
Anti-Tank Battalion 216
tactically-attached *Korück 532* with
    light 102nd and 108th Royal Hungarian Divisions
    Lokot People's Defense

At the end of May 1942 the "von Gilsa" Group, deployed in four combat groups, launched a concentric attack on the partisans from the areas of Brasovo, Lokot, Nerussa, and Negino. During the month of June the partisans were cleared from the villages bordering the forests. On 10 June 1942 Kaminski described the ferocity of the fighting to Headquarters, 2nd Panzer Army in Orel:

"As a result of the events on the nights of 2-3 and 5-6 June, it can be claimed with certainty that the partisans in our rayon have received reinforcements from other rayons. I have never witnessed such a desperate and numerically-strong attack during the entire time I have been fighting against the partisans. The attack was carried out on the entire front line and an attempt was made to cut off our battalions in the front line. The only possible remaining conclusion is that even more fighting will develop in our sector of front. I therefore request that 2 or 3 companies of German soldiers be sent to help me in this partial sector. [...]

Furthermore, Herr General, I wish to report that the partisans all have our armbands with the black cross, which they are able to make easily. They are thus able to approach and we are losing many people. My men must therefore be given uniforms as quickly as possible, something the partisans can't copy."

At the end of June 1942 the battle groups took the offensive in the area of primeval forest south of Briansk. Dense undergrowth, numerous swamps with the associated plague of insects, and a skillful enemy combined to slow the advance by the German troops. Nevertheless, by the beginning of August 1942 partisans had been cleared from a total of 80 villages. When the operation was concluded in September 1942, the von Gilsa group reported the following successes:

- 9,000 partisans and suspected partisans captured
- 4,000 enemy killed
- 200 guns
- 500 machine-guns
- large quantities of explosives and a printing shop

Members of the "von Gilsa" Group remember the time in the Lokot area:

"In addition to the military experience, during those summer months in Lokot the group gained impressions that are probably unique. We got to know the Russian people as friends; we found them capable of tremendous hospitality; we were able to take part in the happy music and dance which they were capable of even in these pitiful conditions."

On 19 July 1942, even while the operation was going on, the commander-in-chief of the 2nd Panzer Army, Generaloberst Rudolf Schmidt,[10] transferred additional *rayons* to Kaminski and bestowed upon him the title of Lord Mayor of a Self-Governed District (SVB). This now encompassed the *rayons* of Mikhailovka, Navlya, Brasovo, Susemka, Dimitrovsk, Dimitriyev, and Komaritschi. As well, Headquarters, 2nd Panzer Army now referred to the Russian volunteer unit as People's Defense Brigade "RONA"[11] and Kaminski as *Brigadekommandeur*, a rank that did not exist in the *Wehrmacht*.

In September 1942 the People's Defense Brigade already had more than 6,000 men, plus eight tanks (KV I and T-34), five armored cars (BT-5 and BT-7), and three armored troop carriers (BA-10 and BA-20). When the group was taken from Gilsa and attached to the 4th Army, the Rübsam Group[12] (H.Q. of the 17th Panzer-Grenadier Brigade) took over the function of a tactical leadership unit in the self-administered district of Lokot.

The Self-Governed District of Lokot

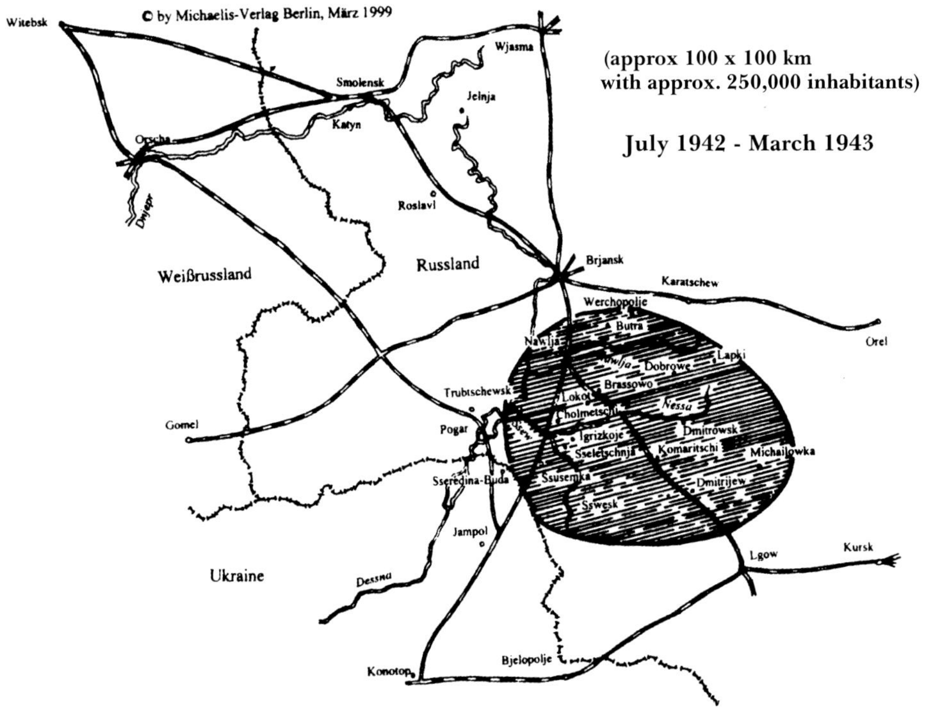

On 5 November 1942 strong partisan units attacked Kokushino (30 km southwest of Lokot). Fifty partisans were killed in the fierce fighting, while the People's Defense lost just two men killed. Thirteen days later the People's Defense destroyed an enemy camp in the forest east of Nevar (40 km southeast of Lokot). At the cost of five wounded, the attackers captured 37 prisoners, 70 cows, 52 horses, and 100 sheep. The partisans lost 48 killed, with 39 rifles and 3,000 rounds of ammunition.

On 14 December 1942 a 300-man-strong partisan unit ambushed the railway station at Komaritschi, killing two German and two Hungarian soldiers and wounding two Hungarians and four Germans. The local People's Defense company blocked the partisans' retreat at Irizkoye (27 km southwest of Lokot) and wiped them out.

After partisans sacked Butre (30 km southeast of Briansk) on 26 December 1942, the People's Defense company from Navlya blocked the bandits' retreat and recovered the stolen goods. Casualties were six wounded, while 11 partisans were killed.

Three days later a company of the People's Defense ambushed a partisan supply column near Orliya (15 km west of Sevsk), and among the goods taken were 80 hundredweight of grain, 30 horses, and 12 cows. A former member recalled another operation against the Soviet partisans:

"For a time the partisans continually mined the roads out of the village, causing numerous incidents resulting in serious wounds or death among the residents of the village. In response, several People's Defense men went into hiding and a few days later they were able to surprise two partisans laying more mines, One partisan was killed in battle, the other was captured. We tied him up and sat him on a stump, then placed his mines around him and set them off. Word of this got around quickly and the partisans became so afraid of us that—if they had a mission, to let's say blow up a bridge—they would simply go into the woods and blow up a few trees, then report their mission accomplished."

After additional *rayons* were placed under Kaminski's command during the summer the People's Defense grew steadily, and even carried out regular recruiting in the villages of the self-governed district. Forced enlistments meant that the fighting value of individual units varied greatly. In addition to highly-motivated members, the companies also contained men who had no interest in fighting or National-Socialist politics. Nevertheless, at that time desertion was not yet a serious problem.

On 31 December 1942, the People's Defense had 13 battalions with a total of about 900 men, organized as follows:

Bn.	Location	Strength	Rifles	Lt. MG	Hvy. MG	Lt. Mortar	Hvy. Mortar	Pistols	SMGs	Artillery/ Anti-Tank
Headquarters	Lokot	343	169	4	-	-	-	110	-	4
I.	Tarasovka	680	525	25	16	7	5	18	2	5
II.	Kholmetsky	720	595	29	19	10	3	37	8	6
III.	Dubrovka	801	696	37	23	26	5	17	8	7
IV.	Lokot	423	395	18	4	-	-	1	-	-
V.	Navlya	984	862	19	15	5	2	41	10	6
VI.	Igritskoye	582	504	14	13	3	-	-	2	2
VII.	Selechnya	718	644	27	14	-	-	-	1	3
VIII.	Dimitrovsk	undergoing reorganization an reformation								
IX.	Dimitriev	446	391	8	2	1	-	-	-	-
X.	Sevsk	undergoing reorganization an reformation								
XI.	Lokot	690	644	23	15	12	-	30	5	8
XII.	Susemka	undergoing reorganization an reformation								
XIII.	Mikhailovka	undergoing reorganization an reformation								
Total		6,387	5,423	205	121	64	15	254	36	42

Also available were 15 armored vehicles, but serviceability was low because of shortages of fuel and spare parts. One former member remembers the mood in Lokot and of the People's Defense men:

"In 1941 there was a great euphoria, even in the district city of Lokot. The population was so grateful that the Stalinist system was over. They put a chamber pot on the head of the Lenin monument in the central square, placed a Soviet gas mask over his face and

slung pieced-together bivouac sheets and a guitar around his neck. As well, many relieved themselves on the seven steps leading up to the monument. What with the summer heat and the many flies it was not a pleasant thing!

Everyone was ready to fight Bolshevism and this explains the initial rapid growth of the People's Defense. Early on, however, the treatment of Russian prisoners and civilians resulting from German policies caused a growing bitterness to rise in the people. When, in mid-1942, we went to the POW camps to recruit Red Army men for the People's Defense, we had little success. Kaminski therefore turned to recruiting young men from the self-governed district for military service. As the Red Army had already conquered part of the self-governed district by the beginning of 1943, morale was not the best. The complete loss of the homeland and the subsequent evacuation to White Russia further heightened this."

In January and February 1943 the People's Defense took part in "Operations Polar Bear I to III," organized by the 2nd Panzer Army. The attacks were directed against the Panshenko Group, a major partisan formation in the Dimitriyev—Mikhailovka area; however, the People's Defense battalions were limited to a screening role towards the north.[13]

At the same time other elements of the People's Defense—namely the 7th Battalion—were seeing action for the first time. Following Army Group B's collapse during the winter of 1942-43, Stalin ordered the "Briansk Front" to roll up the German Army Group Center from the south. On 12 February 1943 the Soviet attack struck the 2nd Army with full force, but ran into a determined defense and gained little ground. The "Central Front" then came to the aid of the "Briansk Front" by

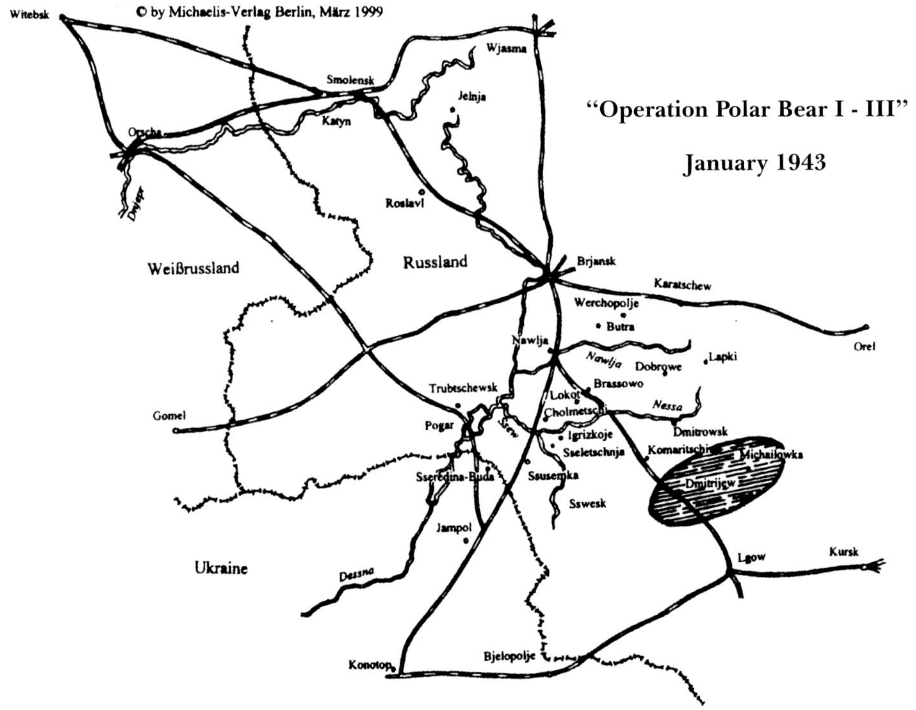

attacking the neighboring 2nd Panzer Army. To counter the enemy advance near Dimitrovsk, elements of the nearby 8th People's Defense Battalion were attached to SS Battle Group Zehender,[14] part of XXXXVII Army Corps. Other elements saw action with the 72nd Infantry Division, part of XX Army Corps. Initially employed for reconnaissance purposes, the battalion was later used to build fortifications.

While the German formations were able to repulse the attacks by both Soviet fronts (army groups) and the Red Army subsequently halted further advances in the Orel area at the end of March, the *rayons* of Komaritschi, Dimitrovsk, Mikhailovka, and Susemka were removed from the self-government district and placed under direct *Wehrmacht* command; they had become frontline zones. As the Soviet Army had conquered the *rayons* of Sevsk and Dimitriyev in the recent fighting, Kaminski's administration had been reduced to the *rayons* of Navlya and Brasovo with about 80,000 inhabitants, of whom 6,575 were refugees from the other *rayons*.

The Self-Governed District of Lokot

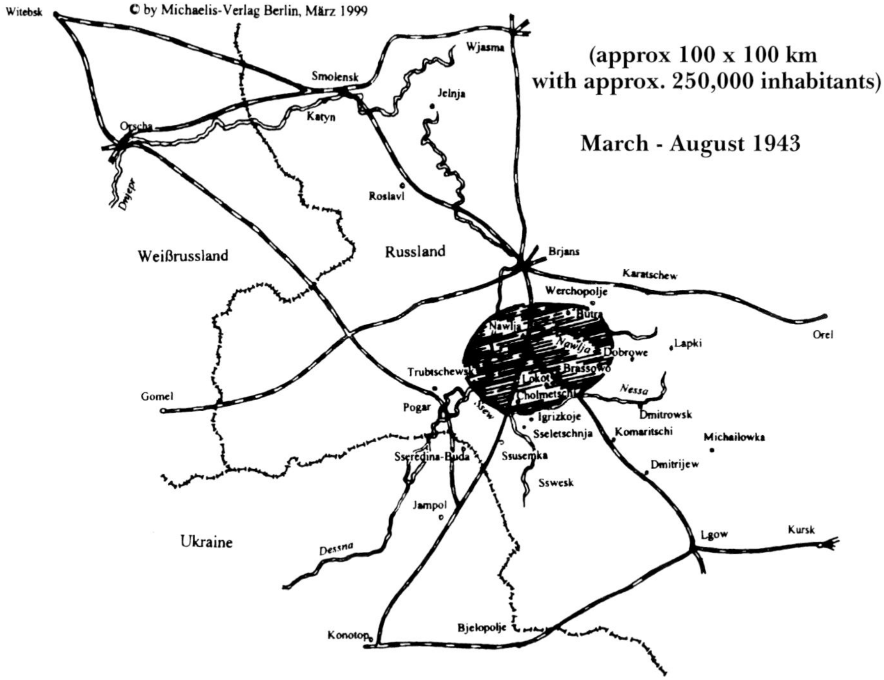

Developments at the front led to chaotic conditions in the rear areas. The behavior of German soldiers toward the Russian population is described in a report by the German liaison staff attached to People's Defense "RONA" in March 1943:

"On 20 March 1943 a group of 850 evacuees from the front (women, old men and children) passed through Lokot. The exhausted women and children, who had just walked 40 kilometers, were weeping, arousing pity among the population. The procession was escorted by German soldiers carrying clubs in addition to weapons. The women said that several

children had died during the march. The escorting soldiers stated that those who collapsed during the march were finished off, and that the transport had numbered more than 1,000 persons when they took it over. The affair caused a sensation among the population. Kaminski was also critical and complained because the evacuees, some of whom were members of the People's Defense, had been mistreated."

This was no isolated case, and *General der Panzertruppen* Lemelsen,[15] in command of the XXXXVII Panzer Corps operating in that area, felt it necessary to issue an order to his subordinate units:[16]

"I demand that the troops be thoroughly briefed that the self-governed district and its institutions exist by order of the Führer and excesses by the troops against the self-governed district are in violation of a directive by the Führer. I will therefore take drastic action against excesses, regardless of person."

The string of successes by the Red Army of course led to great unrest among the population and the People's Defense. The latter began showing serious signs of disintegration for the first time. Secret Field Police Group 639 noted in its activity report in March 1943:

"On 24 February 1943 the 2nd Company of the Russian Karachev People's Defense left its positions and entered the nearby forests to join up with the bandits. On the 26th and 27th almost all of the members of the company returned, except for a few people who had stayed in the forest and had joined the bandits. The seven ringleaders were interrogated by the Karachev detachment and based on its findings Korück 532 sentenced them to death by firing squad. The sentence was carried out on 12 March 1943."

On 22 March 1943 Headquarters, 2nd Panzer Army ordered the destruction of the Red Army troops who had broken through in the most recent battles and the remaining partisan units in the army's rear area. Special Purpose Division Detachment 442[17] (*Generalleutnant* Karl Bornemann[18]) was placed in overall command of anti-partisan operations in the area, and he recommended the withdrawal of the Hungarian divisions, as they were in constant conflict with the People's Defense. The German command's initial response was to withdraw the Royal Hungarian 108th Light Division. This left *Generalleutnant* Bornemann with the following units at his disposal for anti-partisan duties:

Special Purpose Division Headquarters 442
251st and 707th Infantry Divisions
Gruppe Kaellner and Jagdverband Huzel
SS Battle Group "Zehender"
Rübsam Headquarters with
    People's Defense units of the Self-Administered District of Lokot
Royal Hungarian 102nd Light Division
Security forces of Korück 532 positioned on the Desna
Security forces of the XX Army Corps which could be made available

The units were to launch a concentric attack from the north, east, and south, force the partisans in the woodlands south of the Navlya—north of Seredina Buda—Gremyach back against the Desna and destroy them. It was estimated that the time required for this action—independent of weather and road conditions—would be four weeks. The approximately 20,000 men committed to the operation failed, however, to completely liberate the area and destroy the partisans there.

The People's Defense, which to date had worn Soviet uniforms with white armbands bearing the Iron Cross, now began receiving German uniforms to a greater extent. With recruiting potential reduced almost to zero, strength had fallen to about 7,100 men. The brigade's weaponry consisted of:

209 light and 146 heavy machine-guns
82 light, 7 medium, and 7 heavy mortars
24 45-mm anti-tank cannon
21 76.2-mm guns
8 126-mm guns
1 37-mm anti-aircraft gun
1 88-mm anti-aircraft gun
12 tanks
3 armored cars
27 trucks
8 automobiles
440 horses

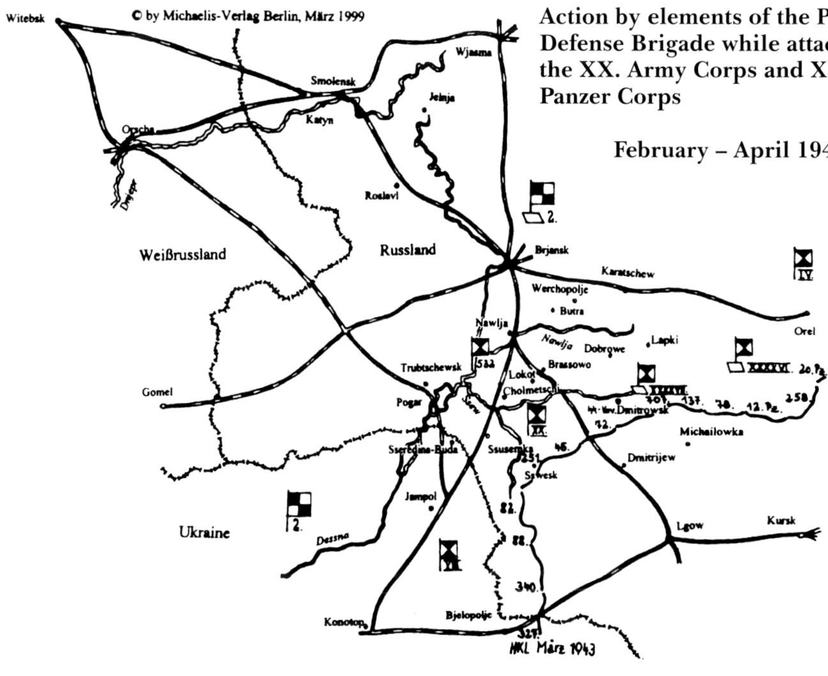

Action by elements of the People's Defense Brigade while attached to the XX. Army Corps and XXVII. Panzer Corps

February – April 1943

The German command was forced to recognize, however, that the People's Defense Brigade was no longer a generally reliable unit. Evidence of this was appearing in the Dimitrovsk area, where the VIII Battalion, deployed in the 72nd Infantry Division's sector of the front (XX Army Corps), was showing signs of disintegration. When, during Easter 1943, all company and platoon leaders and senior NCOs were given leave, the men also left on their own—some never came back. With Dimitrovsk now no longer a part of the self-governed district, Kaminski ordered the battalion moved to Lokot in order to regain control over the men. These wanted to remain with their families in the Dimitrovsk District, however, touching off another wave of desertions. It was only with some difficulty that the soldiers were convinced to leave for Lokot.

Beginning on 16 May 1943, elements of the "RONA" People's Defense Brigade took part in "Operation Gypsy Baron," an anti-partisan operation in the wooded area south of Briansk. Four days later "Operation *Freischütz*" was launched north of Briansk, with the I, II, III, and XI People's Defense Battalions taking part. The most important reason for the two operations was to secure Army Group Center's supply routes in the area of the Orel salient. Two railway lines passed through the area: the single-track section Smolensk—Roslavl—Briansk—Orel and the more capable twin-track section from Minsk to Briansk via Gomel. Five partisan brigades had been identified along the Roslavl—Briansk line and six along the Briansk—Lokot line. These carried out 69 attacks in May 1943, destroying 35 locomotives and 106 rail cars. In the following month the total number of attempts rose from the 675 of the previous month to 841. 298 locomotives were destroyed and 1,222 rail cars damaged and 44 bridges destroyed.

For "Operation Gypsy Baron," Headquarters, XXXXVII Panzer Corps (2nd Panzer Army) had at its disposal approximately 40,000 men from the following units:

7th Infantry Division
292nd Infantry Division
4th Panzer Division
18th Panzer Division
10th Panzer-Grenadier Division
Royal Hungarian 102nd Light Division
security forces of Korück 532
"RONA" People's Defense Brigade
Special Purpose East Battalion

At times there was fierce fighting in the difficult terrain. On 24 May 1943 the OKW War Diary reported that "Operation Gypsy Baron" was gaining ground against at times stubborn resistance. The next day the 18th Panzer Division, in particular, was able to improve its front against the partisans. At the same time, however, a band of approximately 500 men managed to break out to the south through the Navlya position held by the Hungarians. In the days that followed the operation proceeded without serious incident—it was not until 2 June 1943 that another enemy group succeeded in breaking out

Members of the German liaison staff attached to the "RONA" People's Defense Brigade in the summer of 1943.

of the pocket. It was, however, encircled once again 27 km north-northeast of Seredina Buda. The 7th and 292nd Infantry Divisions gained further ground on 4 June 1943. Attempts by the enemy to break out to the east and southwest were repulsed. With the clearing of several wooded areas the operation was considered closed on 6 June 1943. The partisans lost:

3,152 dead
1,568 captured
569 deserters
24 guns
3 tanks
14 anti-tank guns
55 mortars
2 aircraft

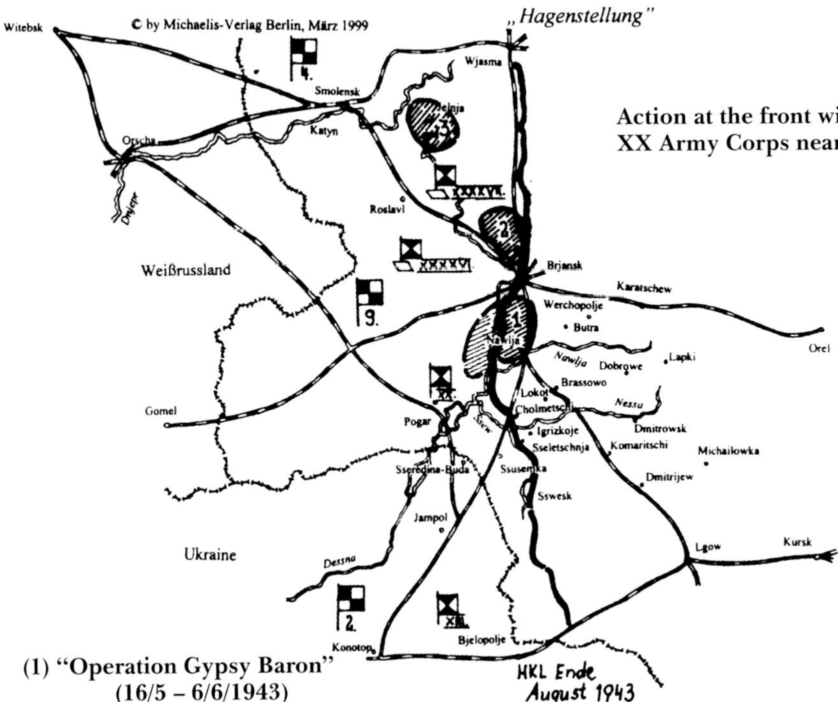

Action at the front with XX Army Corps near Sevsk.

(1) "Operation Gypsy Baron" (16/5 – 6/6/1943)
(2) "Operation Freischütz" (20 – 30/5/1943)
(3) "Operation Seydlitz" (25/6 – 27/7/1943)

"Operation *Freischütz*" was led by Headquarters, LV Army Corps (2nd Panzer Army), and was supposed to pacify the area between the Bolva and the Briansk—Zhukovka line. It was believed that the 3rd Partisan Division as well as the "Orlov" and "Solotuchin" Brigades were present there with a strength of about 6,000 members.

Committed on the German side were approximately 10,000 men of the:

6th Infantry Division
5th Panzer Division
Special Purpose East Headquarters 455
Security Group South with:
- Grenadier Regiment 747 (707th Infantry Division)
- Armored Train 4 (Korück 532)
- Security Battalion 587 (Korück 532)
- Security Battalion 791 (Korück 532)
- People's Defense Battalion III (Korück 532)
- People's Defense Battalion XI (Korück 532)
- Azerbaidzhani Battalion 807 (Korück 532)

Extreme weather conditions (constant rain) made it almost impossible to reach the daily objectives. On 24 May 1943 the encircling ring was held against two breakout attempts and tightened further. There was fighting northwest of Doroshevo and south of Godunovka, during which a heavily-fortified partisan camp complex with bunkers and trenches was discovered. Two days later various encircled partisan units again made several attempts to break out. On 27 May 1943 the troops launched a concentric attack against the mass of the enemy, now squeezed into a confined area. It turned out, however, that there were only about 3,000 partisans instead of the estimated 6,000. By 30 May the entire wooded area was combed once again and then the operation ended. Enemy losses were:

1,459 dead
420 prisoners
6 deserters

With a haul of 193 rifles, 20 submachine-guns, and 33 automatic rifles and total German losses of 27 killed, questions arose about actual combat operations. The numbers for "Operation Gypsy Baron" raised similar questions. It appears that, in part at least, it consisted of nothing less than mass executions of elements of the population identified as "bandit friendly."

Beginning 14 June 1943, XII Battalion of the "RONA" People's Defense Brigade took part in "Operation Tannhäuser." This was followed by "Operation Seydlitz" in the area south of Dorogobush from 25 June to 27 July 1943. At that time the People's Defense Brigade had barely 7,000 men with:

500 machine-guns
40 mortars
30 76.2-mm field guns
10 armored vehicles

After the failed German summer offensive at Kursk ("Operation Citadel") the Red Army succeeded in breaking through 2nd Panzer Army's front. On 26 July 1943 Hitler authorized the abandonment of Orel. The subject of the Russian population and Kaminski came up during one of the related discussions between Hitler and *Generalfeldmarschall* von Kluge,[19] Commander-in-Chief of Army Group Center. Hitler wanted to use evacuated elements of the population to construct the so-called "Hagen Position." This position extended north to south along the Bolva and Desna following the line Kirov—Briansk—Sevsk. Kluge responded by pointing out that the harvest would then be lying in the fields and the employed Russians would constantly leave the construction work. The population of the self-governed district of Lokot was not to be used in any case, as it was being moved to White Russia. *Generalfeldmarschall* von Kluge stated:

"I have directed that he (Kaminski) must not to be touched for the time being, so that we can get the entire trek, which is already on the move, over here through the difficult Desna area. And back here I have active partisans, who have not been killed off, but instead are now rising again, all of a sudden reinforcing everything here again with a huge cover story."

On 4 August 1943 the advance detachments of the Soviet 3rd and 63rd Armies reached Orel. The German forces withdrew to the Hagen Position.

Transfer and Action in the Lepel Self-Governed District

The evacuation of the civilian population from the former self-governed district of Lokot began on 20 August 1943 by way of Seredina Buda, Lukaschenkov, Prokopvka, Novgorod Seversk, Pushkari, and Gramyach to Pogar. While the 4th Regiment of the "RONA" People's Defense Brigade was destroyed in the fighting in the Sevsk area after 26 August while part of XX Army Corps, the remaining people's defense units accompanied the civilian population during their transport by rail from Pogar to Vitebsk. *Oberleutnant* Keiling, commander of the 1st Battery of East Artillery Battalion 621 later awarded the Knight's Cross, recalled the trek:

"The bridge at Peretorgi, which was guarded against partisans and air attack by a battery of East Artillery Battalion 621 made up of Russian volunteers, was so hermetically sealed by an easily-surveyable all-round defensive position that even German generals had to show their pass to the bridge commander before being allowed into the ring to cross the bridge. Units passing through, both large and small, were closely inspected. The security measures were handled strictly according to regulations so as to render pointless any attempt at sabotage.

RONA was no exception in this regard and had to be reported by the responsible officer. Some senior officers wearing the POHA sleeve emblem, cap braid and shoulder boards asked me to come see their commanding officer, but I stayed at my command post as per regulations and also referred these officers and my own ranks to the official procedure, to which even German generals had to submit. Then a Russian, plain looking, but obviously held in high respect by his entourage, stepped forward. He said, 'I am brigade commander Kaminski' and produced a typewritten pass from Headquarters, 2nd Panzer Army, which confirmed that he had been named brigade commander. He then vigorously expressed his indignation over the treatment he had received, and his German liaison officer had to explain to him that he had definitely not been slighted.

The remaining armed members of the RONA stood in stark contrast to the group of officers. They wore pieces of Soviet Army uniforms, sometimes supplemented by civilian things or articles of German service dress. Their equipment and weapons, also of Soviet origin, completed the picture. Tractors towing heavy guns and hose-drawn anti-tank guns were interspersed among the groups carrying small arms. Some groups appeared to be unarmed, so that they could be taken to be prisoners of war. The long rows of wagons and carts of the civilian trek seemed endless."

By the beginning of September 1943 the bulk of the evacuated population and the People's Defense had assembled in the area west of Vitebsk. The arrival of approximately 30,000 people caused more than logistical problems. In particular there were large-scale occurrences of disintegration. In the very first days elements of the VII People's Defense Battalion made contact with the regional partisan command and deserted. On 28 September 1943 the commander of *Einsatzgruppe "B,"* SS-*Standartenführer* Ehrlinger[20] reported his impressions of Kaminski to the head of the anti-partisan units, *SS-Obergruppenführer und General der Polizei* von dem Bach:[21]

"With the disintegration of the army area and the withdrawal of 3rd Panzer Army's border to the south (the new border ran along the southern boundaries of the rayon of Lepel—Shashniki—Senno—Bogushevskoye) the entire area of the self-governed district of Lepel is now the responsibility of Headquarters, 3rd Panzer Army. On the part of HQ, 3rd Panzer Army, the Kaminski matter has been settled as follows:

Territorially, Kaminski's responsibility will be limited to the rayons of Lepel, Shashniki and Ushatshi, of which the latter is still completely controlled by bandits. Within this area Kaminski retains all of his previous rights. Effective immediately, Hauptmann Könnecke's liaison staff is attached to Headquarters, 3rd Panzer Army. The German military administration headquarters and town headquarters are being withdrawn from the Kaminski area. The liaison staff will, however, retain a number of field offices to bolster German ability to maintain supervision.

Following the arrival of Kaminski's people's defense brigade in the district of Lepel, the 286th Security Division, which was in control of the area at that time, undertook to distribute the armed forces in the area. This division was not entirely in keeping with the wishes of Kaminski, who originally intended to concentrate as many forces as possible in Lepel, a measure that would allow him to keep a better watch on his soldiers, who had been more or less uprooted by the resettlement, and reduce their susceptibility to enemy propaganda. From Lepel, he would then conduct various offensives to liberate ever greater parts of the surrounding territory. At present the Kaminski Brigade is in the following locations:[22]

1. Rifle Regiment – Lieutenant-Colonel Galkin23 – road security in strongpoints east of Lepel to Botshekovo.

2. Rifle Regiment – Lieutenant Golyakov, previously Major Tarasov – Senno

3. Rifle Regiment – Major Turlakov – Beshenkovichi and strongpoints from Botscheikovo through Beshenkovichi in the direction of Vitebsk along the road plus field watches on the Ulla.

4. Rifle Regiment – Major Proschin – Lepel with field watches west and north- and southwest of Lepel.

Guards Battalion (fast special-purpose battalion)

Armored Division[24] *– Captain Samsonov – Lepel, only one T 34 tank and one KV I tank are serviceable because of lack of oil.*

The units' armament can be viewed as satisfactory. The only complaint concerns the shortage of ammunition, but here too help is expected. The state of service dress and equipment is slightly better than in Lokot, but still unsatisfactory. Coats and boots in particular are lacking. During the current unfavorable, damp weather and later when the cold arrives, this fact may so reduce the operational capabilities of the units that combat operations outside their bases will become impossible.

The self-governed district's food situation is worse than in Lokot, because the troops must rely almost exclusively on Wehrmacht rations and cannot obtain additional food from agricultural concerns. The Russian soldier's great reliance on adequate bread supply will result in a drop in operational capability and willingness to fight.

At present the mood among the troops is decidedly depressed. The signs of unreliability are piling up; susceptibility to enemy propaganda is increasing. According to the latest information about 300 men have deserted from the unit stationed in Senno. Only determined intervention by deputy Kaminski was able to restore the situation. Kaminski realizes what the effective enemy propaganda means for his men, and he complains about the lethargy and inefficiency of the Lepel propaganda unit which makes planned, convincing counter-propaganda impossible.

Another important factor in the overall situation is that, because of the splitting of his units by Security Division 286, Kaminski is no longer capable of conducting the large-scale operation against the bandits in his area as originally planned. Instead of regiments he can now only deploy battalions. Consequently the planned encirclement of the bandits, which should have resulted in the liberation of at least 50% of the self-governed district, is also out of the question.

Kaminski asserts again and again that he trusts his officers and men. In this respect, however, he is at odds with the generally-held view on the German side.

The morale of the native Russian population has clearly deteriorated since the arrival of the people's defense brigade.

This development is caused by the ongoing conflicts between the refugees from Lokot and the inadequacy of Kaminski's measures. The locals fear for their own safety after the withdrawal of German troops, as the German-sympathetic population has absolutely no trust in Kaminski's people's defense brigade. Typical of the differences between Kaminski and the native population is a speech [given] by Kaminski's propaganda chief at an information meeting in the Lepel movie theater on 23 September 1943, in which he placed the blame for the terrible conditions in Lepel and the bandit movement solely on the local population. Just how badly the locals want German military units to remain in Lepel is illustrated by the rapid spread and exaggeration of rumors to the effect that new German units are already on the way. It is to be accepted as fact that two bicycle companies are being stationed in Lepel."

Headquarters, 3rd Panzer Army also viewed the people's defense brigade as a potential source of danger. In his report on the bandit danger he wrote:

"Rosony is no longer in the army's area, however all the bandits are lined up against Polotsk and the Nevel—Polotsk and Vitebsk—Dünaburg (Daugavpils) rail lines. Bandit strength has grown to more than 11,000 men! Shifts to the west have taken place. The area

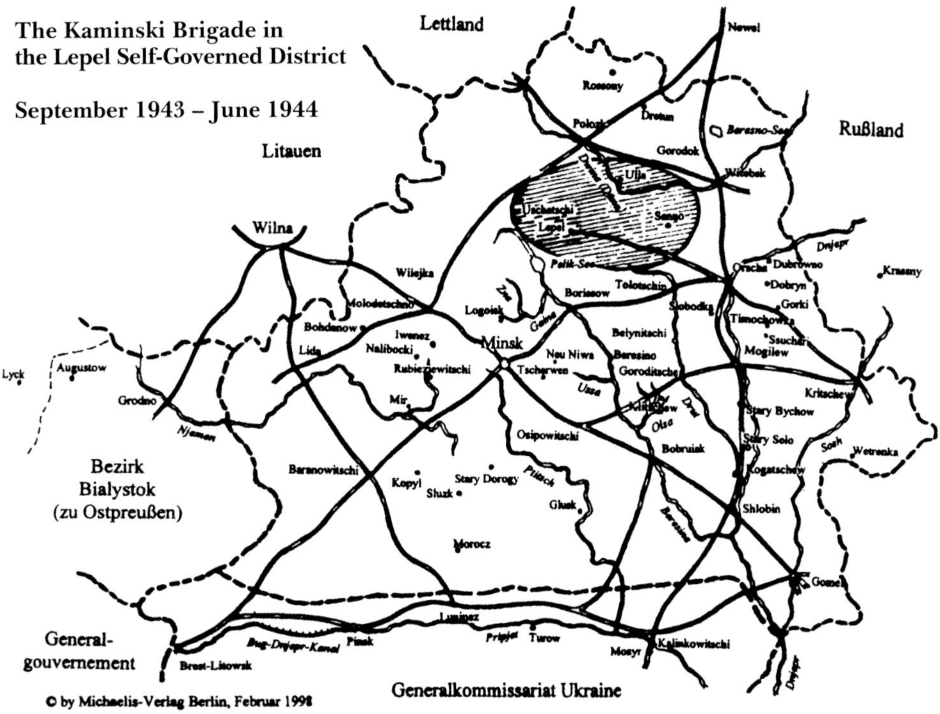

between the Polotsk--Dünaburg rail line and the Latvian border is occupied by bandits; 2 brigades there totaling 1,500 men. It has not been possible to repel all bandit attacks on the Nevel—Polotsk and Polotsk—Vitebsk lines. Insufficient forces! Forward sweeps no longer possible. Further approaches to the tracks and mining of roads.

The Vitebsk—Polotsk—Lepel—Senno area is already controlled by bandits. Maintaining German strongpoints difficult. Total bandit strength in these areas about 15,000 men. Increasingly better armed. Several tanks northwest of Senno! German strongpoints cut off from the outside world. Convoys only on the Vitebsk—Lepel road. Radio communication impossible! Barricades of trees on the road to Lepel. Major attack on Senno believed imminent.

The Kaminski Brigade has moved in with about 6,000 men and 25,000 civilians. Some problems with quartering. Crowding in Lepel causing ill feeling. Alarming desertion of elements of the VII People's Defense Battalion in Senno on 23 September 1943. Assassination attempt planned against Kaminski.

Kaminski intervened very energetically (arrest of officers)! The army expects further appearances of disintegration. Withdrawal of Security Regiment 931. Morale of the People's Defense low. Kaminski remains confident. The army has doubts about this in the long run. Army considers posting of German troops absolutely essential."

"Operation Hubertus" began on 16 October 1943. Its aim was to clear the Senno—Shashniki road, transport the 3,000 remaining residents of Lokot to Shashniki, and liberate most of the Beshenkovichi—Senno—Usvayka River area. Committed were the 2nd, 3rd, and 5th Rifle Regiments,[25] plus the Guards

Areas controlled-- at least partially -- by partisans, with suspected number of same.

Status: January 1944

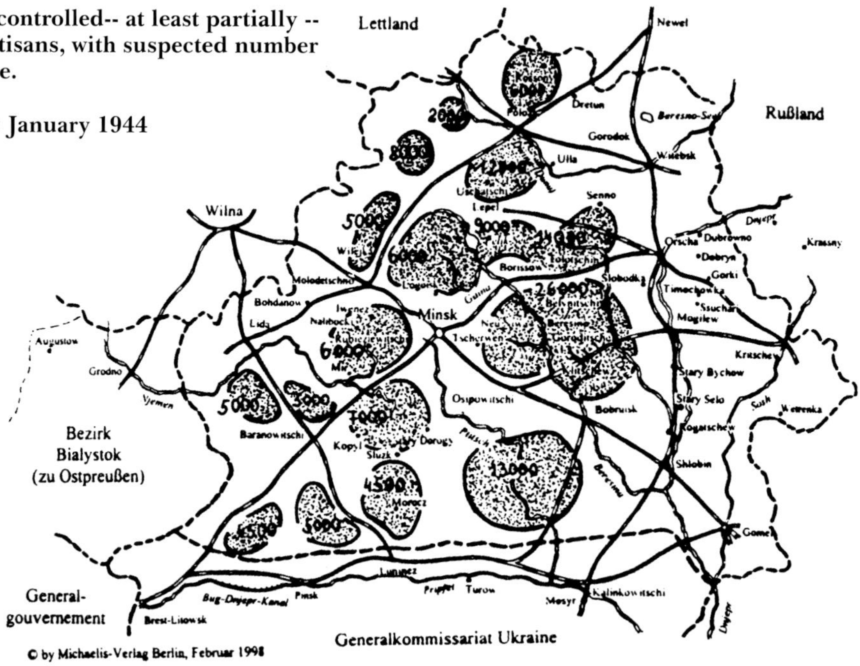

Battalion. After at times fierce fighting, all battle groups arrived back in Lepel on 27 October 1943. The People's Defense had lost 34 killed, the partisans 562. *Hauptmann* Könneke of the German liaison staff wrote of "Operation Hubertus":

"*The People's Defense performed well offensively. Some attacks were pursued with vigor. The quality of the units varied; the personality of the unit commander was always the deciding factor.*

The main fighting power of the People's Defense lies in its tanks and heavy weapons, as the bandits have nothing similar with which to respond.

The People's Defense is less good in defense. The necessary doggedness is missing. Confidence in their own power easily wanes when ammunition is short."

Here again there is a great discrepancy between the losses of the People's Defense Brigade and the partisans. Even if one allows that "successes" are usually exaggerated, here too the question as to the nature of the combats arises again.

At the beginning of January 1944 the Red Army launched its winter offensive against the 18 divisions of the 3rd Panzer Army with 56 rifle and 3 cavalry divisions plus 5 rifle and 22 tank brigades. The 1st Baltic Front halted its offensive after ten days of fighting, having failed to achieve the desired success. After the conclusion of this first battle of Vitebsk, further forces were taken from the already-weak 3rd Panzer Army. Stalin, however, was determined to force a breakthrough at Vitebsk before the end of January, and he ordered the 11th Guards, 4th Shock, and the 5th, 33rd, 39th, and 43rd Armies to launch a

The "RONA" People's Defense Brigade in action in February 1944.

Members of "RONA" with Caucasian volunteers.

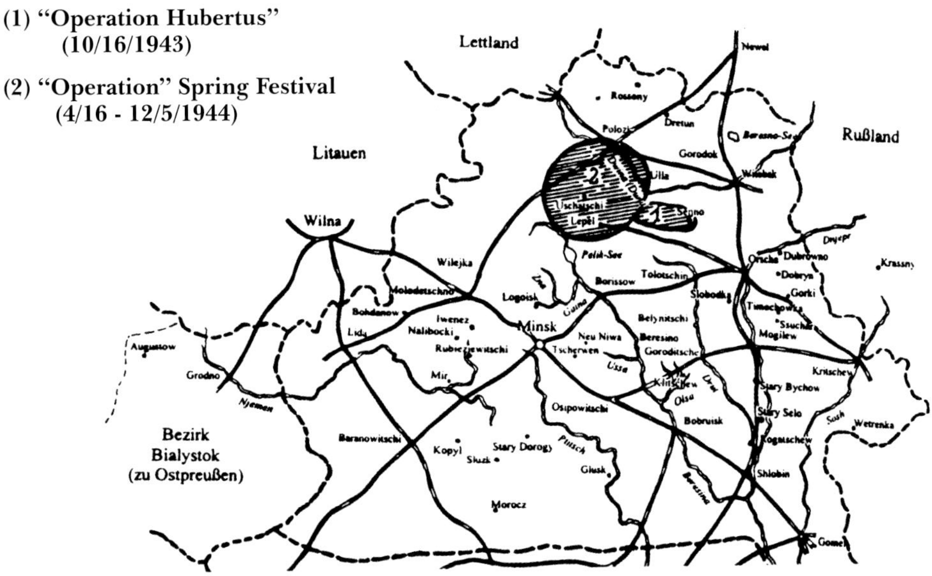

new offensive against 3rd Panzer Army. The Soviet forces were forced to halt their attack in mid-February, mainly on account of heavy snow. Proposals by Army Group Center to either fall back on the Dniepr or to the Beresina were rejected by Hitler. Instead, he ordered that the cities of Bobruisk, Mogilev, Orsha, Vitebsk, and Minsk be turned into "fortified places."

While the German *Wehrmacht* was fighting off fierce attacks at the front, Kaminski was attempting to solidify his position in the new self-governed area and combat the partisans in the 3rd Panzer Army's rear. In both he was only partly successful—it was no longer possible to speak of life in Lokot or the self-governed area. The retreat to Lepel had shattered the morale of the People's Defense and the population—they felt like refugees and suspected that the war was already lost. A former member recalled:

"*The conditions in White Russia were at times chaotic. Some units and officers were in contact with the partisans. The morale of most officers had been shaken. For example, I remember Major Turlakov, who in the winter of 1943-44 was invited to Berlin together with Lieutenant-Colonel Belaj. When he saw the pitiful circumstances and living conditions of the Russian prisoners of war and eastern workers there, he came back broken. In a subsequent discussion with Kaminski he ripped off his shoulder boards and decorations (including the Iron Cross, First Class) and declared that he was probably on the wrong side! Kaminski and I calmed him down, but we were unable to prevent Turlakov from taking his own life in spring 1944 by throwing himself under the tracks of a tank he had been sitting on. One day others hung banners on the houses: `Down with Bolshevism and foreign rule'. Of course the Germans ordered the banners taken down immediately.*"

Generalmajor Heidkämper, chief of the 3rd Panzer Army's general staff, met Kaminski on 16 April 1944:

Celebrating Easter in Kaminski's house on April 16, 1944.

In the center General Staff Oberst Ludendorff with the brigade commander.

In the center Kaminski. Beside him Generalmajor Heidkämper. On the extreme right is General Staff Oberst Ludendorff.

"Today I and several officers of the senior command were invited to join the commander of the RONA in Lepel for the Easter celebration, which is also to be a farewell party for the RONA.

The RONA was originally conceived as an organization of armed farmers. Then last autumn it had to be moved out of the Orel salient with women and children to its new home in the Lepel area, in order to first clear it of partisans. There are approximately 7,000 men under arms, who are soon to take part in our `Spring Festival' anti-partisan operation. Lunch, which began with the famous `sakuska', lasted more than four hours, and the principal drink was vodka. I gave to the commander of the RONA, Herr Kaminski, whose wife I escorted to the table, a gift certificate for an 8-cylinder Horch automobile, a gift from the commander-in-chief (of Army Group Center; author's note) in gratitude for the clearing of the area we are now taking over..."

Also present was the 1st General Staff Officer of the 3rd Panzer Army General Staff, *Oberst* Ludendorff:

"As the Lepel area lay in 3rd Panzer Army headquarters' rear area, Kaminski was frequently in contact with our supply administration section to discuss matters of supply. I met him officially when he and the senior SS and police commander of `White Russia', a General der Waffen-SS von Gottberg[26]*, attended a big conference about an offensive against partisan units in our rear area. Somewhat later I also saw Kaminski when off duty. The first time was at a social evening at the headquarters of a flak brigade attached to us, the second time at his headquarters in Lepel.*

Several officers of the operations and supply sections were invited to Lepel to celebrate the Russian-Orthodox Easter holiday, which falls on the Sunday after our Easter. General Heidkämper and I flew in the Stork to Lepel, about 60 km away, where a lavish lunch with much alcohol was served in the home of Kaminski, who was decorated with the Iron Cross, First Class by the way. Our conversations were translated by interpreters. As the host spoke little German, I didn't speak with him before or after the meal—I wasn't sitting at his table. I did, however, occasionally say `Prost' and when we left late in the afternoon I thanked him for his hospitality. It was very curious that the wives of Kaminski's inner circle, who spoke only Russian, led by Madame Kaminski, took part in the meal and were seated as our partners at table. As conversation with them was impossible, such as there was was conducted among us Germans over them. For their part the women saw to it that we all had enough to eat and drink."

The very next day "Operation Spring Festival" began with:

Operations Group "Krehan" (*Oberst* Krehan, commander of Security Regiment 64)
- Security Battalion 722
- Security Battalion 839
- Regional Defense Battalion 330
- Armored Security Company 350
- 2 companies of Field Fortification Construction Pioneer Battalion 784
- 1 battery of Heavy Artillery Battalion 845 (150-mm SP guns)
- 1 battery of Assault Gun Brigade 245
- Pioneer Battalion 565

Operations Group "Kaminski"
- 1st Regiment
- 5th Regiment
- Guards Battalion27
- 1 battery of 122-mm guns
- 2 batteries of 76.2-mm long-barreled guns
- 1 anti-tank company (8 x 45-mm)
- 1 company of Pioneer Battalion 743
- 1 company of Field Fortification Construction Pioneer Battalion 784
- 1 battery of Heavy Artillery Battalion 845 (150-mm SP guns)
- Organization Todt Unit "Werra" (of the Senior Special Purpose Pioneer Commander 8)

Operations Group "Anhalt" (*SS-Obersturmbannführer* Anhalt, commander of SS Police Regiment 2)
- SS Police Regiment 2
- SS Police Regiment 24
- SS Special Battalion "Dirlewanger"[28]
- Police Battalion 62
- 1st and 3rd Batteries of Police Gun Battalion I
- 1 battery of Police Artillery Battalion 56
- Headquarters and 1 company of Pioneer Battalion 743
- 1 combat team (3 x 37-mm and 3 x 20-mm) of the Flak Battalion "Command Staff RF-SS"
- 1/2 canine battalion

Operations Group Rehdantz (commander: *Major der Schupo.* Weissig, commander SS Police Regiment 26)
- SS Police Regiment 26
- Police Battalion 57
- reinforced Security Service battalion
- III Battalion/Police Rifle Regiment 31
- 1 company of the Special Purpose Rural Police Operational Detachment
- 1 battery of Police Battalion 57
- 1 battery of SS Police Regiment 26
- 3 batteries of the 201st Security Division
- 1 company of Field Fortification Construction Pioneer Battalion 730
- 1 combat team (3 x 37-mm and 3 x 20-mm) of the Flak Battalion "Command Staff RF-SS"
- 12th Police Armored Company
- 1/2 canine battalion
- II Battalion/Police Rifle Regiment 36
- 20-man TN company as special mines clearing team

Battle Group Jeckeln: (commander *SS-Oberführer* Panzinger)
5th Latvian SS Frontier Guard Regiment
III Battalion/SS Police Regiment 16
Latvian Police Regiment 2
Latvian Police Regiment 3
elements of the 281st Security Division
Field Fortification Construction Pioneer Battalion 730
Field Fortification Construction Pioneer Battalion 731

The fighting in the Ushatshi area lasted until 12 May 1944. Casualties on the German side were 175 killed and 625 wounded. Enemy losses totaled 3,654 dead and 1,794 captured. Once again the question arises, whether this numerical relationship was the result of combat operations or executions.

While 40% of the "RONA" People's Defense Brigade took part in "Operation Spring Festival," in mid-April 1944 those elements not involved escorted the population by rail to Dyatlovo (south of Lida). In mid-May the elements that had been involved in "Operation Spring Festival" also arrived there and were attached economically to the SS and Police Commander "Bialystok." A former interpreter remembered conversations between *SS-Obergruppenführer und General der Polizei* von Gottberg and Brigade Commander Kaminski:

"One day Obergruppenführer und General der Polizei von Gottberg came to Dyatlovo from Minsk to see Kaminski. The latter was planning a Russian self-administration there like the one in Lokot. Von Gottberg wanted nothing to hear of a self-governed area. I was interpreter during this discussion, although Kaminski spoke reasonably good German. It went something like the following: as well as the Soviet partisans, the Polish Home Army (Armija Krajowa) was already fighting in this area. To the Germans they were all bandits and they wanted Kaminski to also fight against the Poles. Kaminski categorically refused, however. Von Gottberg screamed at him and I translated without toning down the expressions. Kaminski responded in kind—with Russian curse words. I translated, but toned down the expressions. Kaminski finally won out—at least for the moment. The RONA would not have to fight the Poles."

Concerning this, a former staff officer of the "RONA" remembered:

"It is correct that Kaminski was determined that the RONA should not fight against the Armija Krajowa. His fight was against Stalin and bolshevism, not against the national struggle of the various peoples. His slogan was: against communism and foreign rule. This, of course, was not what the Germans had in mind.

Kaminski declared that he had long ago abandoned enmity between Russia and Poland and he did not want to contribute to further problems. He would not commit his RONA against nationalist Poland!"

When the Red Army resumed its westward advance and on 28 July 1944 reached the western border of the USSR at Brest-Litovsk, the "RONA" People's Defense

Brigade Commander Kaminski with Oberst der Schutzpolizei Weissig at a briefing during "Operation Spring Festival".

Bronislav Kaminski, decorated with the Iron Cross, First and Second Class, the Wound Badge in Black, and the Medal of Bravery for Members of the Eastern Peoples First Class in Gold. Beside him is Oberleutnant Alexei Bagaturia, platoon leader in a "RONA" transport company.

Operational conference prior to "Operation Spring Festival".

Second from left: Oberst der Schutzpolizei Weissig, Brigade Commander Kaminski and far right Oberstleutnant Shavykin.

Brigade and the civilian population were moved farther west. The question arose as to where and how the approximately 21,000 civilians were to be housed and fed. After numerous discussions it was finally planned to evacuate civilians to Pomerania and the members of the people's defense brigade and their families (about 10,000 people in total) to Hungary.

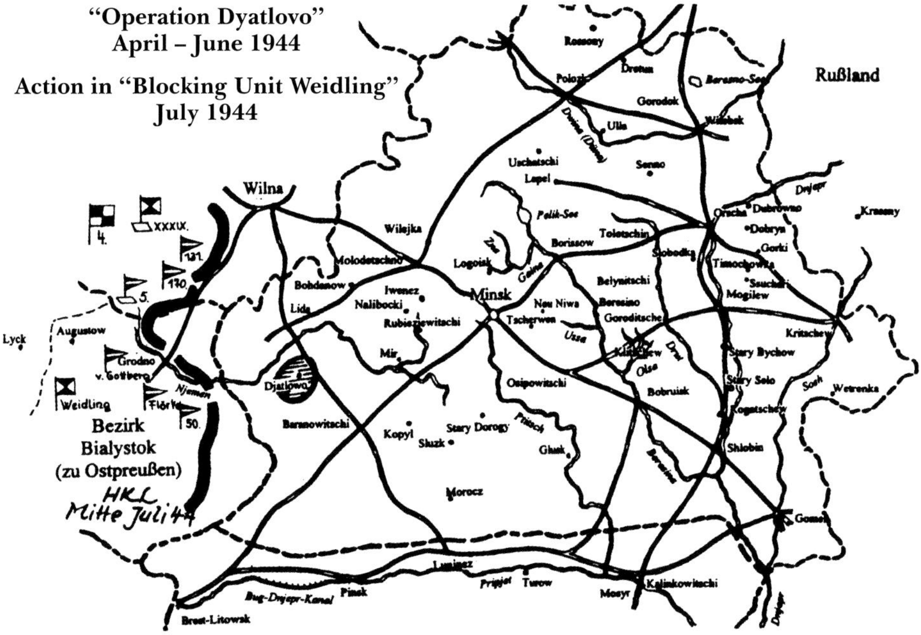

SS Waffen-Sturmbrigade "RONA"

Always interested in an expansion of the *Waffen-SS*, *Reichsführer-SS* Himmler and *SS-Obergruppenführer und General der Waffen-SS* Berger,[29] head of the SS Central Office in Berlin, began to take an interest in the people's defense brigade. One of the officers working in the newly-established *Freiwilligen-Leitstelle "Ost"* (Central Office for Volunteers East) under *SS-Obersturmbannführer* Dr. Fritz Arlt[30] was *SS-Obergruppenführer und General der Polizei* von Gottberg. During his service as commissar-general of White Ruthenia and Senior SS and Police Commander "Central Russia and White Ruthenia" he had had frequent contact with Kaminski and the "RONA" People's Defense Brigade in the Lepel area. Concerning this, Army Group Center noted on 29 May 1944:

"As of late the Kaminski movement, principally in the area of Army Group Center, has been closely watched and taken care of by the SS (SS-Obergruppenführer Gottberg in Minsk). At present the top leaders have no intention of bringing about a thorough clarification of this matter. Most of all they want to wait for the further development of the Kaminski movement."

Just fourteen days later, however, the order was issued for the takeover of the people's defense brigade by the *Waffen-SS*! On 17 June 1944 it was issued Military Post Office Number 45 155 as *Waffen-Sturmbrigade der SS "RONA."* While the *Wehrmacht* liaison detachment was withdrawn, *SS-Sturmbannführer* Reußner replaced *SS-Hauptsturmführer* Loleit as *Waffen-SS* liaison officer. A former member of the RONA recalled:

"Reußner was a kind and sympathetic man who was probably sent to us because they couldn't use him anywhere else. When Kaminski recommended him for promotion to SS-Obersturmbannführer and the Iron Cross, First Class Reußner was the happiest man!

Reußner spoke little Russian, and his interpreter—a Baltic German SS-Obersturmführer with an excellent knowledge of Russian—translated everything. Reußner was especially proud of his Blood Order—he always had photographs in his pocket showing Hitler presenting him with the order and visiting him in the hospital. In the summer of 1944 I asked him what he was going to do at the end of the war—it was already quite obvious that the war was lost. His answer was simply idiotic: the Russians are socialists, he was a National-Socialist, in reality they were all socialists and they would work something out. His predecessor Georg Loleit—first an SS-Obersturmführer and then SS-Hauptsturmführer—was different. He came to us in Lepel as Waffen-SS liaison officer and was a repugnant, arrogant fellow. I didn't see him again until the Ratibor area. Loleit came from Estonia, just like another SS-Untersturmführer who was there. The third member of the group was an ethnic-German SS-Oberscharführer from Russia. All three spoke fluent Russian. Loleit survived the war and was living in the Stuttgart area in 1946."

From the approximately 3,000 remaining men, a new type *SS-Sturmbrigade* (assault brigade) was to be formed with a grenadier battalion (4 companies) and a heavy battalion (one each of infantry gun, anti-tank, flak, and pioneer companies).

The planned reorganization was initially delayed, however, by the Red Army's summer offensive, which began on 22 June 1944. Within a few days the Soviet army had smashed Army Group Center. Vitebsk was encircled and subsequently fell on 27 June. Hitler's order to turn Vitebsk into a "fortified place" had resulted in 10,000 German soldiers becoming prisoners of war, while countless others had died in the ruins of the city. The next day the remnants of the 3rd Panzer Army withdrew into the area of the former self-governed district of Lepel. The resulting gap between Army Groups Center and North could not be closed. Leaving their heavy weapons behind and losing equipment in the swamps, single German battle groups tried to make it to the west. On 29 June 1944 the Soviets reached the Beresina.

Just three days later enemy units cut the Minsk—Molodechno road, while other Soviet formations coming from Bobruisk arrived south of Minsk. When Soviet tanks advanced on the White-Russian capital from the north, elements of the 4th Army (28 divisions with approximately 350,000 men) still flooding back across the Beresina were encircled east of Minsk.

Lithuanian Vilna (Vilnius), a "fortified place" in 3rd Panzer Army's area and boundary between the 3rd and 4th Panzer Armies, was supposed to halt the Soviet offensive. Positioned south of Vilna was the XXXIX Panzer Corps with the 131st and 170th Infantry Divisions. To its south was "Blocking Unit Weidling" 31, which included the 5th Panzer Division, Battle Group "von Gottberg," Battle Group "Flörke," and the 50th Infantry Division.

A battle group was formed from elements of the *Waffen-Sturmbrigade der SS "RONA,"* still designated a People's Defense Brigade, in the Dyatlovo area. For several days it was attached to Battle Group "von Gottberg" and the 50th Infantry Division. From 4 July 1944 the men repulsed numerous partisan attacks from the Nalibocka Forest between Lubcz and Nieniewicze. Fighting against regular units of the Soviet army followed in the line Wsielub and Novogrodek (southeast of Lida) until 8 July. While the German battle groups were forced back towards the Grodno area within a few days, the Russians were pulled out of action and followed the units and families, which were by then in the Tschenstochau area.

The *29. Waffen-Grenadier-Division der SS "RONA"* (*russische Nr. 1*)

The plan to move the *Waffen-Sturmbrigade "RONA"* to Hungary together with family members had meanwhile been abandoned. The German command instead now planned to place the approximately 10,000 people in Slovakia. The relationship between the Russian and Slovakian languages was a decisive factor in the decision, as was the potential partisan threat in Slovakia. Because of the pace of events the transports were initially stranded in different areas. Thus, in July troops and civilians found themselves in the Tschenstochau, Cracow, and Ratibor areas. Getting the families of his soldiers to safety was now seen by Kaminski as his most urgent task. At the end of the month at Rastenburg, Himmler appointed him

Waffen-Brigadeführer and commander of the new *29. Waffen-Grenadier-Division der SS*. A former officer recalled:

"On 30 July 1944 Kaminski drove to Rastenburg with chief-of-staff Lieutenant-Colonel Shavykin and the chief intelligence officer. The next day there, Kaminski was named Waffen-Brigadeführer and commander of the 29. Waffen-Grenadier-Division der SS "RONA" (russische Nr. 1), which was to be established shortly. During the personal conversation between Himmler and Kaminski, Himmler—still feeling the effects of the attempt on Hitler's life just ten days earlier—said that he would dearly love to have a bodyguard made up of RONA members. We then received our new rank badges from the SS clothing stores in Berlin. Shavykin was a former Red Army captain and had served under Kaminski as a platoon leader. In the RONA he rose to chief-of-staff and was given the rank of a lieutenant-colonel. One can have mixed feelings about his military abilities, but he had Kaminski's trust..."

Also present during these conversations was *SS-Obergruppenführer und General der Waffen-SS und Polizei* von dem Bach,[32] who presented Kaminski with the Anti-Partisan War Badge. On 2 August 1944 he wrote in his diary:

"I saw the RF-SS again the day before yesterday and I also met Guderian. Also present was Kaminski, leader of the Russian volunteer corps, with whom I had to conduct lengthy negotiations."

The *29. Waffen-Grenadier-Division der SS "RONA" (russische Nr. 1)* was to be established at the Neuhammer troop training grounds in Silesia as a new-style infantry division, with:

Waffen-Grenadier-Regiment der SS 72 (russische Nr. 1) – 2 battalions
Waffen-Grenadier-Regiment der SS 73 (russische Nr. 2) – 2 battalions
Waffen-Grenadier-Regiment der SS 74 (russische Nr. 3) – 2 battalions
Waffen-Artillerie-Regiment der SS 29 (russische Nr. 1) – 4 battalions
SS-Füsilier-Bataillon 29 (fusilier battalion)
SS-Pionier-Bataillon 29 (pioneer battalion)
SS-Panzerjäger-Abteilung 29 (anti-tank battalion)
SS-Nachrichten-Abteilung 29 (signals battalion)
SS-Versorgungs-Regiment 29 (supply regiment)
SS-Veterinär-Kompanie (veterinary company)
SS-Sanitäts-Kompanie 29 (medical company)
SS-Feldersatz-Bataillon 29 (replacement battalion)

In order to reach the authorized strength of about 11,300 men, in his capacity as the new commander of the Replacement Army the *Reichsführer-SS* planned to integrate the numerous evacuated Russian units—in particular police units and eastern battalions—into the division.

While *Waffen-Brigadeführer* Kaminski and his officers were driving back to Silesia from Rastenburg, Himmler went to Posen, and on 3 August 1944 gave his oft-quoted speech to the district leaders (*Gauleiter*) there. In it he mentioned the people's defense brigade:

"Three of my units escaped the collapse at Minsk or behind Minsk. One was the Russian Kaminski Brigade with 6,000 or 7,000 men, led by a Russian. I had to listen to my German operations staff tell me how many cigar boxes of Iron Crosses the Russians picked up as souvenirs along the wayside because they had been thrown away!"

Although the division existed only on paper at this time, the strategists in the OKW were already planning how to use it. The following entry appears in the war diary of the Commander-in-Chief West under 4 August 1944:

"Order for transfer of the 29. and 30. Waffen-Grenadier-Division der SS (russische Nr. 1 and 2) into the area of the Commander-in-Chief West for anti-terrorist operations (divisions are currently involved in putting down the uprising in Warsaw: strength 6,000-7,000 and 9,000 men). Further orders from the Chief Intelligence Officer."

With almost all deployable elements of the new *29. Waffen-Grenadier-Division der SS "RONA" (russische Nr. 1)* committed in Warsaw and the formation of the division thus delayed for an indefinite period, only the *30. Waffen-Grenadier-Division der SS (russische Nr. 2)* was transferred to the west.[33] Aside from that, *Waffen-Brigadeführer* Kaminski rejected any operations against the western Allies, as his fight was only against Stalin and bolshevism.

Involvement in the Warsaw Uprising

At 1700 hours on 1 August 1944 the Polish Home Army (*Armija Krajowa*—AK) launched an uprising in Warsaw. It was initiated by the Polish government in exile in London, which feared for its position in a postwar Poland. It had been decided that the Poles themselves would liberate the city from German occupation and not the Red Army, which was already on the east side of the Vistula. The Polish rebels initiated a hopeless struggle—with totally inadequate planning and coordination—in every quarter of the city. In the 63 days to follow, it would cost the lives of more than 200,000 people. Nowhere were the Poles able to achieve a decisive success. The vital bridges over the Vistula remained in German hands, as did all other strategic objects. In the Ochota district, Colonel Grzymala ordered an assault on the police barracks in the Academy House on Narutowicz Square. This attack was also unsuccessful. During the night of 2 August 1944 Colonel Grzymala and about 700 lightly-armed members of the AK pulled back into the Chojnow Forest, about 15 km to the south.

SS-Obergruppenführer und General der Waffen-SS von dem Bach, who as Commander of Anti-Partisan Units was responsible for putting down the uprising, was informed of the uprising by telephone in Danzig-Zappot on 2 August 1944. In his diary he wrote:

"Big mess in the General Government."

While still in Danzig he ordered the transfer of the following units to Danzig:

SS Special Regiment "Dirlewanger"
16 police companies of the SS and Police Commander Posen (2,750 men)
"Special Unit Bergmann" (5 officers, 677 Azerbaidzhani volunteers)
Security Regiment 608 (20 officers and 598 men).

As well, the nominal *Waffen-Sturmbrigade der SS "RONA"* in Tschenstochau was placed on alert. *Waffen-Sturmbannführer* Frolow, the chief of operations, formed the following units from approximately 7,000 men:

Waffen-Grenadier Regiment der SS 72 (russische Nr. 1) with 2 battalions
13th (Infantry Gun) Company with two Soviet 122-mm guns
14th (Anti-Tank) Company with eight Soviet anti-tank guns
a tank company with four T-34s and a Soviet assault gun.

On the same day the chief of operations (Ia) of Army Group Center advised the operations officer of the 9th Army:

"1 regiment of SS-Sturmbrigade RONA (Kaminski Brigade) is being sent from the Tschenstochau area. Details of departure and mode of transport (vehicle or rail) not yet determined."

A former member recalled of *Waffen-Sturmbannführer* Frolow:

"Ivan Frolow (age-class 1915) had been a captain and career officer in the Red Army and was captured by the Germans in 1941. In 1942, with the aid of Russian civilians, he escaped from a transit camp for officers and made contact with the RONA in Lokot. There he was made a Major and chief of operations. In August 1944, in Kaminski's absence, he commanded the elements committed in Warsaw, and following the disbandment of the Waffen-Grenadier-Division der SS 'RONA' (russische Nr. 1) he served in the headquarters of the 600th Infantry Division (Russian) and finally in the 650th Infantry Division (Russian). As far as I was later able to find out, at the end of the war Frolow made his way to Czechoslovakia and from there reached Munich. The Polish Secret Service was on the hunt for him there on account of his actions in Warsaw, and one day he 'disappeared', never to be seen again.

As I see it, we only committed 170 men and 60 replacements in Warsaw, not 1,700 men and 600 replacements!"

On 2 August 1944, at 1625 hours, *SS-Obersturmbannführer* Reußner reported to *Major* Völkel that the Russian regiment had reached Rakow (south-southwest of Warsaw). Völkel, 9th Army's operations officer and responsible for coordinating the first counter-operations, advised that it was planned that the Russians should clear the district of Ochota.

For the attack planned for 5 August 1944, *Waffen-Grenadier Regiment der SS 72 (russische Nr. 1)* was reinforced through the addition of 2nd Company, Anti-Tank Battalion 743 with 12 anti-tank guns and 1st Company, Armored Pioneer Assault

Battalion 500 and was incorporated into the "Reinefarth Group." Of this the 9th Army's war diary noted:

"*SS-Gruppenführer Reinefarth has taken over command of all the forces, already committed and yet to arrive, which are to put down the uprising, providing they are deployed against the city from outside. At present the Wehrmacht commander of Warsaw cannot leave the city; command of the attack from inside appears inadvisable.*"

The "Reinefarth Group" (*SS-Gruppenführer und Generalleutnant der Waffen-SS und Polizei* Reinefarth[34]) was organized into three attack groups:

South:	*Waffen-Grenadier Regiment der SS 72 (russische Nr. 1)*
Center:	SS Special Regiment "Dirlewanger" Special Unit "Bergmann" elements of the "Posen Group"
North:	elements of the "Posen Group" 1 battle group from the SS Officer School Brunswick
Reserves:	Security Regiment 608 "Hermann Göring" Field Replacement Battalion 6 companies of military police

According to the 9th Army's war diary, the SS Brigade "Siegling" was also being sent. This fits a report by the Commander-in-Chief West to the effect that the *30. Waffen-Grenadier-Division der SS (russische Nr. 2)* was still being sent to crush the Warsaw uprising. In fact, it was transported directly to France on account of its high potential unreliability.[35]

Waffen-Grenadier-Division der SS 72 (russische Nr. 1)'s attack in Ochota began at 0800 hours on 5 August 1944. Advancing from the southwest on Radomer Street, the regiment crossed Narutowicz Square and reached the University Quarter at Academy Square. Of this, the 9th Army's war diary recorded polemically:

"*Kaminski Regiment, from the south on the Reich Road, has drunk its way up to the Machorka Factory.*"

An important point in this first day of operations is the radio message sent by the reinforced SS regiment to the "Reinefarth Group" at 1726 hours:

"*5,000 captured civilians at Point 27. Request immediate transport out.*"

The numerous executions of Polish rebels and civilians in the first days have been verified. Blame for them is often laid on the Russian members of the *Waffen-Sturmbrigade der SS "RONA."* This radio message proves, however, that the Poles were handed over to other units. Based on eyewitness statements, a Polish committee investigating German war crimes determined that regiment was

Warsaw: the bridge over the Vistula to Praga.

Waffen-Brigadeführer Kaminski at a meeting with SS-Brigadeführer and Generalleutnant der Polizci Reinefarth in Warsaw.

The fighting in Warsaw reduced the city to ruins.

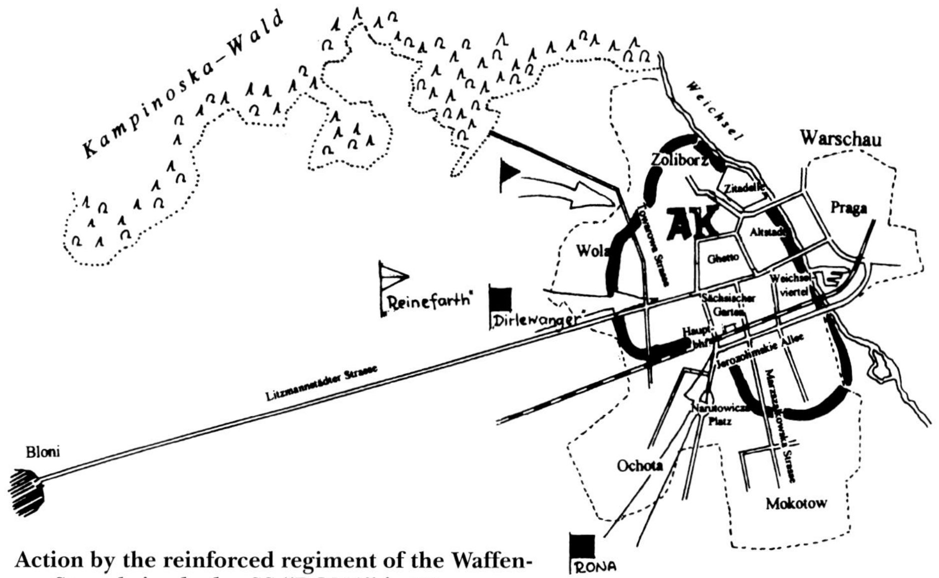

Action by the reinforced regiment of the Waffen-Sturmbrigade der SS "RONA" in Warsaw

5 to 27 August 1944

© by Michaelis-Verlag Berlin, Oktober 2002

probably responsible for "only" 300 murdered civilians. The men were, however, accused of widespread plundering and rape.

That same day *Waffen-Brigadeführer* Kaminski traveled from Rastenburg to Warsaw with *Waffen-Obersturmbannführer* Shavykin in order to convince *SS-Obergruppenführer und General der Waffen-SS und Polizei* von dem Bach to pull his regiment out. As at Dyatlovo, Kaminski did not want to commit his men against the *Armija Krajowa*, and he had no desire to see them sacrifice themselves in the streets of Warsaw. Bach agreed on condition that a replacement for the regiment would arrive. Kaminski initially remained in Warsaw, and from there directed the regiment's operations together with Frolow.

Because of an authorization to plunder, probably issued by Himmler, the Russians' discipline quickly deteriorated and command was scarcely still possible. On 8 August 1944 the 9th Army war diary recorded:

"The Commander-in-Chief feels obliged to direct a request to SS-Obergruppenführer Bach-Zelewski, whom the Reichsführer-SS has placed in overall command of the Warsaw action, to see to it that, given its known fighting style, the Kaminski group under all circumstances avoids excesses against ethnic Germans, such as have unfortunately occurred recently when individual Germans found themselves outside the military strongpoints in the city."

And on 10 August:

"The Kaminski group is still fighting in Ochota; at present, however, it appears to view plundering as more important than continuing the attack."

The following entry appeared in the 9th Army's war diary the next day:

"Kaminski huge failure, today they raped German KdF girls.[36] Our pillaging directive is making itself felt uncomfortably."

On 10-11 August *Waffen-Grenadier-Regiment der SS 72* reached the area Towara Street—Jerozolimskaja Ave.—main railway station—Poznanska Street—Emilia Plater Street. As of 17 August the Russians—bolstered by 600 men from Tschenstochau—were attached to the newly-formed Battle Group "Rohr." *Generalmajor* Rohr thus commanded:

Wehrmacht emergency units (max. 5,000 men)
Flak and ground personnel of the Warsaw airport (approx. 1,000 men)
Waffen-Grenadier-Regiment der SS 72 (russische Nr. 1) (1,700 men)
Geibel Group: units of uniformed regular police and security police as well as *Wehrmacht* emergency units and remnants of the SS Cavalry Replacement Battalion (max. 5,000 men).

The reports on the SS regiment were not without consequences. The former chief of the Army General Staff, *Generaloberst* Guderian, wrote of this in his memoirs:

"What I experienced there was so shocking that I felt obliged to speak to Hitler about it the same evening and demand the removal of both brigades [Kaminski's and Dirlewanger's, author's note] from the Russian front."

In reading this, one can detect certain resentments against the *Waffen-SS* on the part of the *Wehrmacht*. Certainly the numerous foreign units deployed in Warsaw under army command (e.g. Cossacks or Azerbaidzhanis) were no less brutal than these two SS units, and it can be proved that the numerous mass executions were not carried out by members of the RONA!

Throughout the fighting the Kampinoska Forest northwest of Warsaw was of special strategic significance to the Polish Home Army and was a serious operational threat for the German forces. On 23 August 1944 the 9th Army's war diary recorded:

"Rear areas with large concentrations of bandits are: the Kampinoska Forest north of Blonie, where it is believed there are 5,000 bandits, which is receiving a steady stream of refugees from Warsaw, and the forests south of Tomaczow, in which have gathered about 6,000 rebels who are said to have received orders from the AK command to move in the direction of Warsaw...

Given the total number of bandits in the army area of 12,000-13,000 men, we must expect a steady deterioration in the security situation for which the available forces are totally inadequate."

The following entry appeared in the war diary the next day:

"A blocking line has been established northwest of Warsaw to screen against bandit forces trying to enter the city from the Kampinoska Forest."

After the German command had decided to pull the Russian SS regiment out of Warsaw, the 9th Army planned to employ it in the blocking line against the Kampinoska Forest. On 27 August 1944 the 9th Army's war diary recorded:

"The army high command proposes to conduct the screening of Warsaw to the northwest against the entry of bandits from the Pusza Kampinoska offensively, using the regiment of the Kaminski Brigade previously deployed in the southern part of the city, thus ending its employment in Warsaw."

While the members of the RONA moved northwest through the western outskirts of Warsaw, *SS-Obergruppenführer und General der Waffen-SS und Polizei* von dem Bach ordered *Waffen-Brigadeführer* Kaminski to Litzmannstadt, supposedly for a conference. In fact, it was a drumhead court-martial against the increasingly unpopular Kaminski. The following entry appeared in Bach's war diary on 28 August 1944:

"Evening to Litzmannstadt to attend the drumhead court-martial of Kaminski."

In Litzmannstadt Kaminski, together with his driver, chief-of-staff Shavykin, and division medical officer Dr. Sabora were placed under arrest and shot the same day. The bodies were first buried and later burned. After the war a former SS officer declared:

"In connection with the activities of the SS special detachment I also remember an incident in which Bothmann, Bü., R. and B. drove to Litzmannstadt to shoot several SS officers in the local ghetto, it could have been 4 to 6 people, who were allegedly members of a special detachment in the General Government. Even I, the leader of the detachment, was not told why this was being done... The SS officers shot in the ghetto were also later burned in the Kulmhof Forest. A senior SS officer rewarded everyone who took part in this act with 100 extra cigarettes and several bottles of schnapps."

In 1945 a Jew who had survived imprisonment in the ghetto told a Polish examining magistrate that one day in the summer of 1944 a vehicle had been ordered from Kulmhof (Chelmno) to Litzmannstadt. In the late morning hours the vehicle returned to the camp with four bodies, and they were not Jews. The bodies were first buried on the grounds of the palace, and then the next day they were dug up and burned in the forest.

In order to avoid causing further unrest in the "RONA," the German command decided to spread the rumor that Kaminski had been murdered by Polish partisans. A former staff officer remembers this version:

"Kaminski, with Shavykin and our division medical officer, left Warsaw in his Horch, which had been given to him by the commander-in-chief of Army Group Center in Lepel. Accompanied by two Kübelwagen each carrying five grenadiers, the vehicles were forced to slow down in a wooded area and there were ambushed and shot up by Polish partisans.

I visited the scene of the incident myself and saw the three vehicles sitting in a police barracks in Cracow. They were all completely shot up.

When, about a week later, I visited SS-Obergruppenführer von dem Bach and told him of Kaminski's disappearance, he was quite obviously moved. I even believe he had tears in his eyes.

I was present when he issued the order to all police stations between Warsaw and Cracow to report when Kaminski had passed where. This was to enable him to reconstruct the incident."

The behavior of the former *SS-Obergruppenführer und General der Waffen-SS und Polizei* toward the RONA staff officer clearly shows the slyness of the commander of anti-partisan units.

Disbandment of the Division

The uprising in Warsaw held up formation of the division. When *Waffen-Brigadeführer* Kaminski drove to Warsaw, *Waffen-Obersturmbannführer* Belaj was responsible for the units not in action. A former member recalled of him:

"Georg Belaj (year-class ca. 1917) had been an NCO in the Red Army and in 1941 found himself in the Briansk pocket. As he was from there, he simply went home and met Voskoboynik and Kaminski. As he had Kaminski's confidence, he was gradually promoted to Oberstleutnant. At the beginning of August 1944 Belaj was promoted to Waffen-SS-Obersturmbannführer by Himmler, however when he was taken into the 600th Infantry Division (Russian) he went in with the rank of Leutnant and commanded an infantry platoon."

After Kaminski had been shot, SS headquarters installed the former SS and police commander of Lvov (Lemberg), *SS-Brigadeführer und Generalmajor der Polizei* Diehm,[37] as temporary division commander. One month later *SS-Obergruppenführer und General der Waffen-SS* Berger tasked *SS-Gruppenführer und Generalleutnant der Polizei* Jürs[38] with command of the *29. Waffen-Grenadier-Division der SS "RONA" (russische Nr. 1)*. Jürs was to reorganize the division in the German protective zone in Slovakia and from there conduct operations in central Slovakia.

At the end of September 1944 the then not unknown Karl Albrecht—author of the book *Betrayed Socialism*—visited the Russian units on Berger's behalf. After the war Albrecht wrote a rather arbitrary and muddled version of what occurred:

"But Hitler and Himmler had ensured that they had absolutely no military reserves left and could only offer this Kaminski Brigade [to put down the Slovakian uprising]. And then I arrived with this bad news [about the condition of the brigade]. Was he [Berger] supposed to do without these, as he had been told, 10,000 [in fact about 2,500] well-disciplined soldiers? It was a tough battle that he had to fight. I saw this and made a suggestion: I would check out the Kaminski Brigade on his behalf and determine its tactical military worth as well as its moral disciplinary qualities.

General Berger agreed. That same night he called SS headquarters in Berlin and spoke to Himmler, who agreed to dispatch SS-Gruppenführer und General der Waffen-SS Lührs [correctly Jürs], whom I was to meet in Breslau or Kattowitz. Two days later I met Lührs in Breslau. As soon as we spoke I realized that Himmler had instructed Lührs to give a favorable report on the Kaminski Brigade no matter what.

I was unable to agree with Lührs. […] We met again at the office of the SS commander in Kattowitz. The latter already had experience with the brigade, which was quartered in his area of responsibility. I did not know then that Kaminski was already dead, shot. While inspecting the camp, I heard that just prior to our visit his people had found his car in an isolated place, empty with a large pool of blood in the back seat. They believed that partisans had ambushed their general and carried him away! They were still looking for him when Gruppenführer Lührs and I carried out our inspection. The brigade had also played havoc in the Kattowitz area, plundering, raping and mistreating the population, exactly as had happened for years at Briansk and Smolensk.

I said frankly to Lührs that the brigade was a wild band of robbers, the worst kind of bandits, the officers a consortium of cunning rogues and murderers. Lührs laughed: you have to prove that. Furthermore here's an order from Heinrich Himmler that you and Berger have to obey. What's more, I would be careful about expressing such opinions if I was shortly to be the guest of this brigade.

I later heard that Himmler had considered Lührs to succeed the shot Kaminski as an SS-Obergruppenführer und General der Waffen-SS in the event that he successfully prepared the brigade for operations in Slovakia.

I didn't see Lührs again until the banquet given him and his aides in a gaily-decorated hall in brigade headquarters by the acting commander of the brigade Belajef, who wore the uniform of an SS-Standartenführer. Lührs accepted, laughing. I refused. I had already inspected the `brigade' camp and had seen everything I needed to be able to render an objective judgment. […]

I first spoke with the women I met in the camp. […] I talked with wounded who were hobbling around. […] No trace of discipline, of military obedience, of soldierly subordination. […] Many of the people had been recruited forcefully into the brigade. They cursed the day they had joined this band of murderers and wished only for an opportunity to escape. […]

We watched Herr Lührs' parade from the Wagenburg and when it was all over we slowly walked toward the officers standing in front of the large officer's mess.

`Ah, there you are Albrecht. This is a wonderful unit, this discipline, these clear commands, this march pace, this soldierly bearing. You should have seen it.' I just looked at Lührs. […]

I couldn't listen to it all any longer. It was high time for me to disappear. Submachine-guns at the ready, we walked to our cars and drove back to Pressburg [Bratislava] as fast as we could go.

Then I described these frightful things to Obergruppenführer Berger. My adjutant confirmed everything I had said. Berger was appalled. He had never heard anything like it. That same evening a courier delivered my written report to Himmler with the request that he not employ such criminals in an operational role. At the same time Berger demanded that this brigade of bandits be transported to the troop training grounds at Münsingen, where they should be disarmed and brought to accounts. […]

Of course there were also decent, sober men in this `unit', primarily those who had been forcibly recruited and could not run away because of the frightful terror."

With the unit non-operational in its current condition, the *Reichsführer-SS* decided to disband it. Himmler had changed his plans in recent weeks. Always wanting to raise new large formations, following a conversation with General Vlasov,[39] on 16 September 1944 he ordered the formation of the 600th and 650th

Infantry Divisions (Russian). He simultaneously named Vlasov commander-in-chief of the Russian Liberation Army, or "ROA." Himmler directed that all smaller Russian units be transported to the Münsingen troop training grounds for the formation of these new divisions. Included were the approximately 2,000 uprooted RONA members, some of them in chaotic conditions, but who still had twelve T-34 and two KV-I tanks.

At the Münsingen troop training grounds the men were remustered, clothed, and trained for three months. Under *Oberstleutnant* Artemyev the bulk of them formed Grenadier Regiment 1602. The remaining approximately 300 officers were checked out and were given back their original Red Army ranks. Most of those who had been non-commissioned officers became NCOs again. In the end the number of RONA officers was still.[78]

On 6 March 1945 the 600th Infantry Division (Russian) left Münsingen and marched via Weissenburg and Herzogenaurach bei Erlangen (20 March 1945) to Lieberose, arriving there on 26 March. On 13 April 1945 the 1st Battalion of Grenadier Regiment 1602 (Major Solontavin) unsuccessfully tried to crush the Soviet bridgehead over the Oder at Erlenhof from the north.

Saying that he did not want to be drawn into Germany's inevitable defeat, *Generalmajor* Bunyatshenko,[40] the willful division commander, gave orders that the attack on Erlenhof not be repeated. Instead he ordered his division to march south into the Protectorate of Bohemia and Moravia. The *Wehrmacht* lacked the means to intervene.

What the opponents and skeptics had always feared was coming true: the fully-equipped Russian division was becoming a source of danger of the first order behind the German lines. On 18 April 1945 the division marched through Kamenz, and on the 29th was in Teplitz-Schönau (Sudetenland). On 5 May the unit reached Prague and joined the side of the Czech rebels, falling on the rear of German forces. Coming from the southwest, Grenadier Regiment 1602 reached the city center and drove back a counterattack by troops of the *Waffen-SS*. As a result, on 7 May 1945 Prague was, for the most part, in Czech-Russian hands. When the first Soviet troops under Marshall Konev reached the city from the east, the new Czech National Council dropped a bombshell, declaring that it wanted nothing to do with "*traitors and mercenaries of the Germans.*" Faced with this turn of events and the opposing Red Army, Bunyatshenko changed his mind again and tried to get his division to the American lines.

General Vlasov, who was with the division, came upon U.S. troops in Pilsen and unsuccessfully tried to negotiate an agreement for the ROA units not to be turned over. On 11 May 1945 the 600th Infantry Division (Russian) laid down its arms in Schlüsselburg. The next day Vlasov and Bunyatshenko tried to meet with the Americans again, but on the way there they were captured by Red Army troops. Both men were hanged in Moscow on 1 August 1946.

The former RONA members suffered the same fate as the other Russian volunteers who had fought as part of the German armed services: they were sentenced to years of forced labor or death. Only a few succeeded in escaping to build new lives in the west.

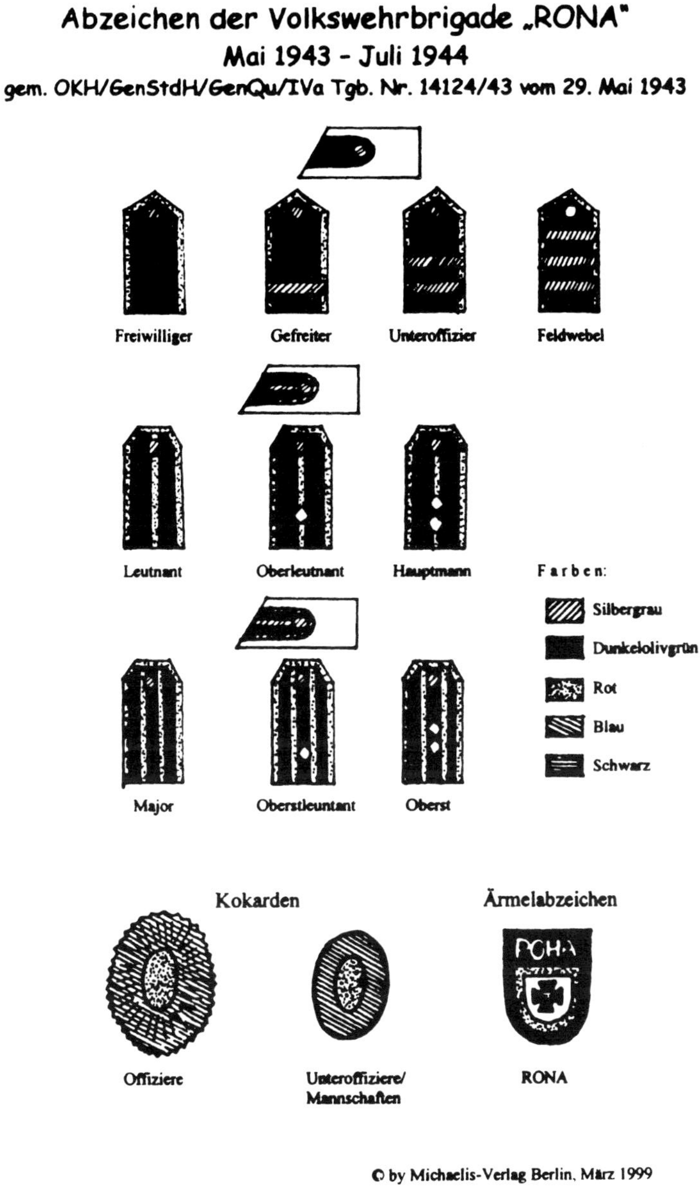

Insignia of the People's Defense Brigade "RONA"

May 43 – July 44

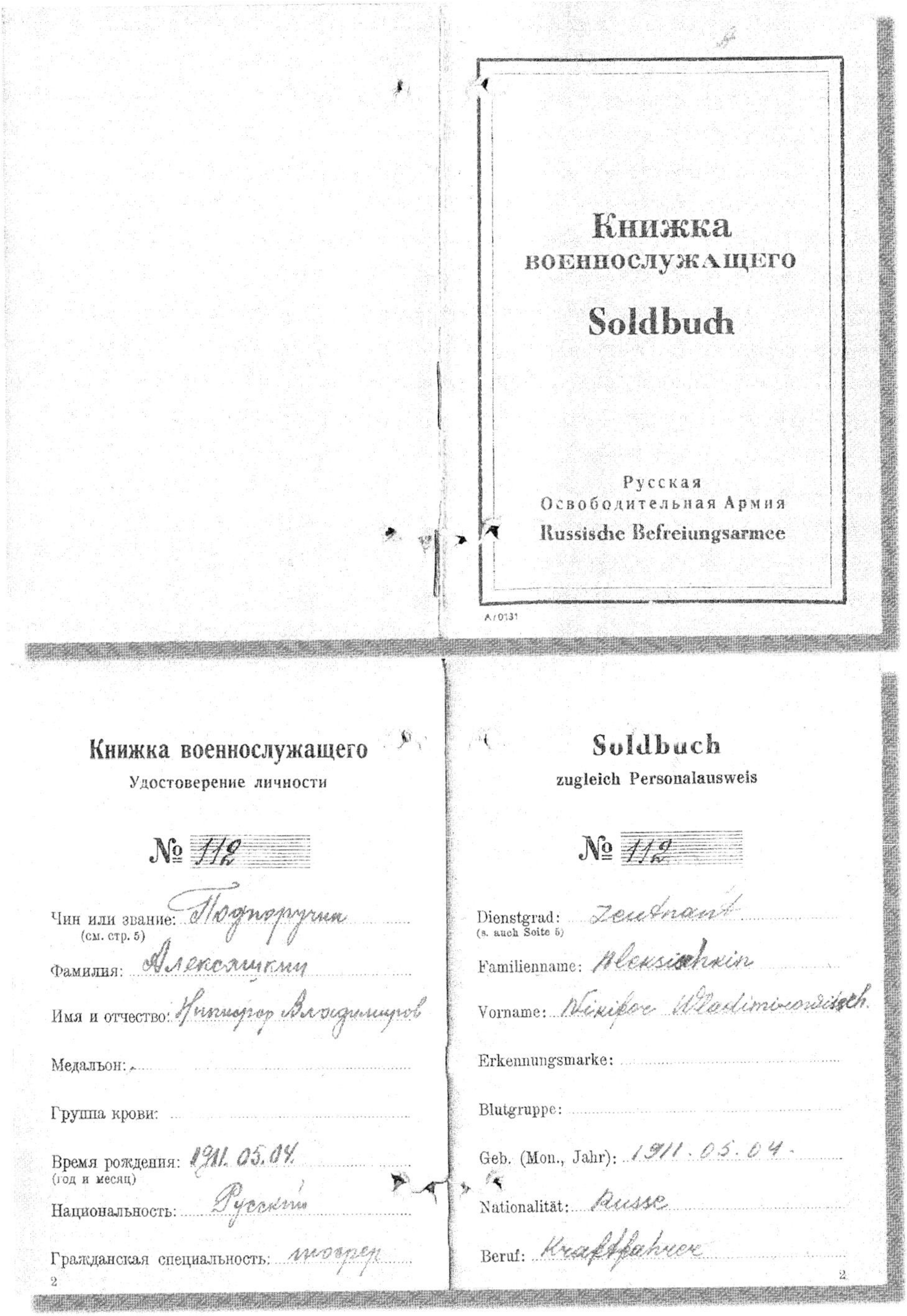

Книжка военнослужащего

Soldbuch

Русская Освободительная Армия

Russische Befreiungsarmee

A/0131

Книжка военнослужащего

Удостоверение личности

№ 112

Чин или звание: Подпоручик
(см. стр. 5)

Фамилия: Алексишкин

Имя и отчество: Никифор Владимирович

Медальон:

Группа крови:

Время рождения: 1911. 05. 04.
(год и месяц)

Национальность: Русский

Гражданская специальность: шофер

2

Soldbuch

zugleich Personalausweis

№ 112

Dienstgrad: Leutnant
(s. auch Seite 5)

Familienname: Aleksischkin

Vorname: Nikifor Wladimirowitsch

Erkennungsmarke:

Blutgruppe:

Geb. (Mon., Jahr): 1911 . 05 . 04 .

Nationalität: Russe

Beruf: Kraftfahrer

2

The paybook of Leutnant Aleksischkin. He joined the People's Defense Brigade "RONA" on 21 January 1942 and after its disbandment joined the 600th Infantry Division (Russian) at the end of 1944.

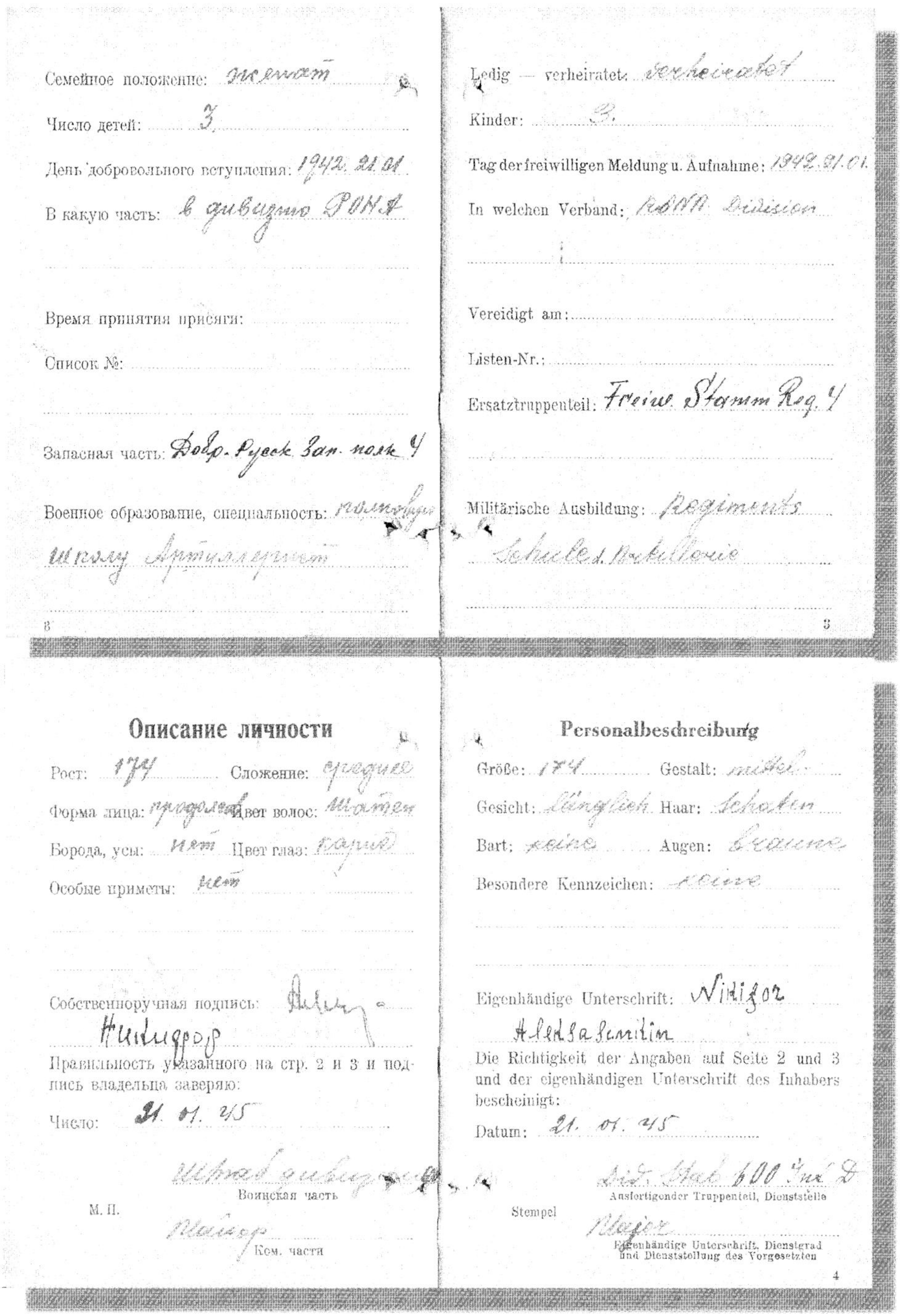

Семейное положение: женат

Число детей: 3

День добровольного вступления: 1942. 21.01

В какую часть: в дивизию РОНА

Время принятия присяги:

Список №:

Запасная часть: Добр. Русск. Зап. полк 4

Военное образование, специальность: полковую школу Артиллерист

8

Ledig — verheiratet: verheiratet

Kinder: 3.

Tag der freiwilligen Meldung u. Aufnahme: 1942. 21.01.

In welchen Verband: RONA Division

Vereidigt am:

Listen-Nr.:

Ersatztruppenteil: Freiw. Stamm Reg. 4

Militärische Ausbildung: Regiments Schule f. Artillerie

3

Описание личности

Рост: 174 Сложение: среднее

Форма лица: продолгов. Цвет волос: шатен

Борода, усы: нет Цвет глаз: кариe

Особые приметы: нет

Собственноручная подпись: Никифор

Правильность указанного на стр. 2 и 3 и подпись владельца заверяю:

Число: 21. 01. 45

Штаб дивизии

Воинская часть

М. П.

Майор

Ком. части

Personalbeschreibung

Größe: 174 Gestalt: mittel

Gesicht: länglich Haar: schaten

Bart: keine Augen: braune

Besondere Kennzeichen: keine

Eigenhändige Unterschrift: Nikifor Aleksa Semilin

Die Richtigkeit der Angaben auf Seite 2 und 3 und der eigenhändigen Unterschrift des Inhabers bescheinigt:

Datum: 21. 01. 45

Div. Stab 600 Inf. D

Ausfertigender Truppenteil, Dienststelle

Stempel

Major

Eigenhändige Unterschrift, Dienstgrad und Dienststellung des Vorgesetzten

4

The *30. Waffen-Grenadier-Division der SS ((russische) Nr. 2)*

The 30th SS Waffen-Grenadier Soviet (Russian No. 2) was no new formation like the 29th SS Waffen-Grenadier Division "RONA" (Russian No. 1) with so-called "SS volunteers," rather it was created by renaming an existing unit and incorporating various other elements. To provide the reader with more in-depth information, an explanation of these formations follows.

It is extremely interesting that the following units were not always purely Russian or White-Ruthenian. In relation to the various nationalities that lived in White Russia, there were White Ruthenians of Polish, Ukrainian, and Russian origins: in 1569 White Ruthenia became part of the Kingdom of Poland through the newly-created "Lublin Union." In the first division of Poland in 1772 the area east of the Dvina and the Dniepr went to the Russian Empire. The area west of Minsk—Pinsk—east of Ternopol followed in the second division in 1793. In the third division of Poland in 1795 the area east of the Neman and Bug Rivers was ceded to Russia. Poland was reborn as a sovereign nation after the First World War. In 1920 British Foreign Minister Curzon proposed the so-called Curzon Line, which took nationality conditions into consideration, as the eastern boundary. In the Polish-Russian war of 1920-21, however, the Poles, exploiting the internal political turmoil in Russia, seized parts of White Ruthenia and the Ukraine (184,000 km^2), even though only 15% of the population there was Polish. In 1937 the majority of those living in the eastern part of White Ruthenia (White Russian SSR) were Russians or White Ruthenians, with Poles, White Ruthenians, and Ukrainians predominating in the west and south. In September 1939 the Red Army reoccupied the former Russian areas, and when the *Wehrmacht* marched into the country in the summer of 1941 the population there was approximately 75% White-Ruthenian, 12% Polish, 10% (Greater) Russian, and 3% Ukrainian. In 1943, during the German retreat from Russia, other nationalities, including many Cossacks and Caucasians, were evacuated to White Ruthenia.

The Police Battalions of the Senior SS and Police Commander "Central Russia and White Ruthenia"

Decisions concerning the administration of occupied eastern lands were made prior to the start of the Russian campaign. Three SS and Police commands were created to secure and pacify these areas and deal with other police matters: "A" (*SS-Obergruppenführer und General der Polizei* Jeckeln) for Army Group South; "B" (*SS-Gruppenführer und Generalleutnant der Polizei* Prützmann) for Army Group North; and "C" (*SS-Gruppenführer und Generalleutnant der Polizei* von dem Bach) for Army Group Center.

Initially these commands had only German police battalions at their disposal. A few weeks after the start of hostilities with the USSR, however, it became apparent that the German forces of the Order Police were inadequate—both numerically and qualitatively—to secure the rear areas. Consequently, volunteer police auxiliary units were soon formed using Baltic, Russian, and Ukrainian volunteers. Most of the volunteers were former policemen, prisoners of war, or other local inhabitants.

Senior SS and Police Commander "C" began his work in Mogilev in September 1941. Renamed Senior SS and Police Commander "Central Russia" in summer 1942, on 21 February 1943 he was transferred to Minsk. When the General Commissariat of "White Ruthenia"[41] with the SS and Police Commander "White Ruthenia" were added to the command on 1 April 1943, the title finally became Senior SS and Police Commander "Central Russia and White Ruthenia."

By order of the *Reichsführer-SS* and Chief of German Police, the foreign police auxiliary units were designated police units (*Schutzmannschaften*) effective 6 November 1941. In addition to individual officers serving in the country and cities, there were complete units, designated police battalions, which were frequently used in the anti-partisan role.

The battalions in the area of the Senior SS and Police Commander "Central Russia and White Ruthenia" were supposed to receive the numbers 44-100. Until the summer of 1944 the position had under its command:

- White Ruthenian Police Battalions 46 and 47. Established in Minsk in July 1942, they were employed as guard battalions until disbanded in the summer of 1944.

- White Ruthenian Police Battalion 48. Also formed in Minsk as a guard battalion in July 1942, but in 1943 it went to the Slonim area as a frontline battalion. The battalion was disbanded in East Prussia effective 1 September 1944.

- White Ruthenian Police Battalion 49. Formed in Minsk in September 1942, it was also employed as a guard battalion there.

- Police Battalion 51, formed from Ukrainian personnel in September 1942. It was disbanded in May 1943.

- White Ruthenian Police Replacement Battalion 53. It was formed in Mogilev in August 1942.

- Police Battalion 54, formed from Ukrainian personnel in Vitebsk in September 1942. It was disbanded on 17 September 1943.

- Police Battalion 55. Formed in September 1942, it was occasionally employed together with SS Police Regiment 14.

- Police Artillery Battalion 56. It was established in September 1942 and was often attached to the SS Special Battalion "Dirlewanger." For example, on 4 January 1943 the battalion took part in "Operation Franz." In August 1944 elements of the battalion formed SS Artillery Battalion 30.

- Ukrainian Police Battalion 57. The unit was formed in Horoditschka in September 1942, and beginning on 4 January 1943 it took part in "Operation Franz," and from 15 January 1943 in "Operation Harvest Festival." "Operation Hornung" followed, beginning on 7 February 1943, then "Operation Lenz South" on 30 March and "Operation Lenz North" on 7 April. The unit later took part in "Operation Hermann," which began on 7 July 1943, and "Operation Spring Festival," which commenced 11 April 1944. On 11 April 1944 the battalion commander, *Hauptmann der Polizei* Siegling, was awarded the German Cross in Gold for the successful operations. In June 1944 the battalion was incorporated into the 1st Regiment of Police Brigade "Siegling."

- White Ruthenian Police Battalion 60. Formed in September 1942, it was assigned a military postal number in April 1944. In June 1944 the battalion was incorporated into the 1st Regiment of Police Brigade "Siegling."

- Ukrainian Police Battalion 61. It was created by renaming and transferring the former Ukrainian Police Battalion 115. From its new base in Slonim, the unit took part in "Operation Spring Festival" beginning 11 April 1944. In June 1944 the battalion was incorporated into the 2nd Regiment of Police Brigade "Siegling."

- Ukrainian Police Battalion 63. This too was a renaming, of the former Ukrainian Police Battalion 118 based in Novogrodek. In June 1944 the battalion was incorporated into the 2nd Regiment of Police Brigade "Siegling."

- White Ruthenian Police Battalion 64. Formed in Glebokje in February 1944, in June 1944 it was incorporated into the 2nd Regiment of Police Brigade "Siegling."

- White Ruthenian Police Battalion 65. Formed in Novogrodek in February 1944, in June 1944 it was incorporated into the 3rd Regiment of Police Brigade "Siegling."

- White Ruthenian Police Battalion 66. Formed in Slutsk in February 1944, in June 1944 it was incorporated into the 3rd Regiment of Police Brigade "Siegling."

- White Ruthenian Police Battalion 67. Formed in Vileyka in February 1944, in June 1944 its personnel also joined the 3rd Regiment of Police Brigade "Siegling."

In March and April 1944 the Senior SS and Police Commander "Central Russia and White Ruthenia" ordered that all Cossack and Caucasian refugees fit for military service be brought together in *de facto* police battalions. The Cossacks formed Cossack Mounted Battalions 68 and 72 to 74, and were supposed to be combined in the Cossack Brigade "White Ruthenia" (two regiments each of two battalions). The German retreat prevented this from happening, however. Instead, the Cossacks were separated. While Cossack Mounted Battalion 68 took part in "Operation Kormoran" in the area north of the Minsk—Borisov railway from 22 May to 20 June 1944, engaging enemy forces that had escaped "Operation Spring Festival," and in June 1944 became part of Police Brigade "Siegling," in June 1944 Cossack Mounted Regiments 72 to 74 assembled in the Siedlce area with their families. Altogether there were about 9,000 men fit for military service and 8,000 civilians. The Cossack mounted battalions were initially employed to guard workers constructing fortifications on the Narev and then were moved with their families into the Trieste area.

Caucasian Police Battalions 70 and 71, also formed in March 1944, were also assembled in Siedlce and then moved to the Isonzo Valley with approximately 2,000 family members.

Police Battalions 52, 58, 59, 69, and 75-100 were not established.

On 9 July 1944 Major Müller, the officer responsible for the Cossack refugees, reported to the East Ministry in Berlin that the White Ruthenian order service had been moved to Neuhammer, in Silesia, and there, in agreement with the general responsible for volunteer units, they were to be assigned to German divisions as foreign auxiliaries.

Paybook of a member of the 118th Police Battalion, which on 22 December 1943 was renamed the 63rd Police Battalion. From 13 October to 6 November 1944 the man belonged to SS Field Police Company 17. He subsequently returned to the 30. Waffen-Grenadier-Division der SS (russische Nr. 2).

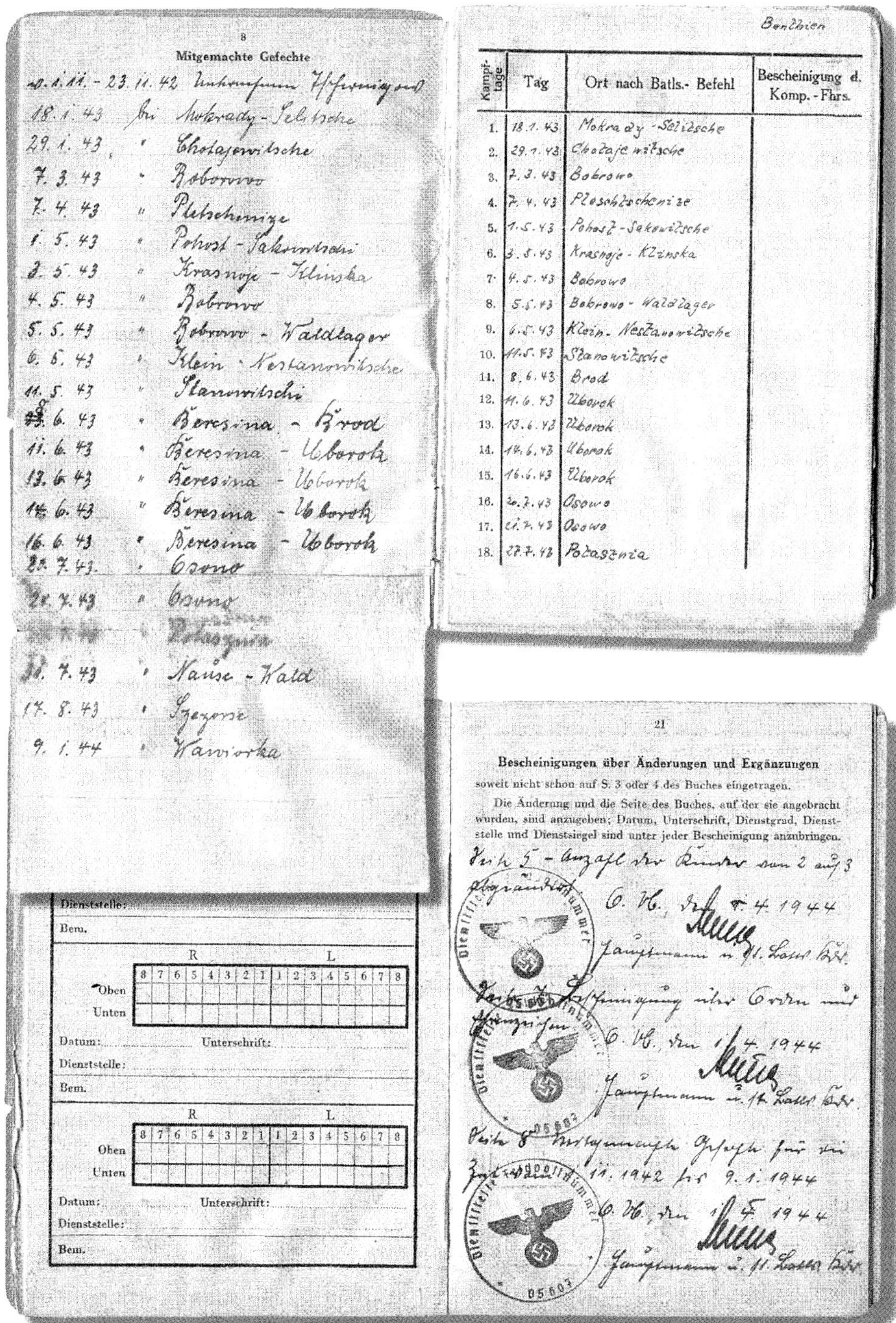

8

Mitgemachte Gefechte

1.11.-23.11.42 Unternehmen Ischerniza(?)
18.1.43 bei Mokrady-Selitsche
29.1.43 " Chotajewitsche
7.3.43 " Bobrowo
7.4.43 " Pletschenize
1.5.43 " Pohost-Sakowitschi
3.5.43 " Krasnoje-Klinska
4.5.43 " Bobrowo
5.5.43 " Bobrowo-Waldlager
6.5.43 " Klein-Nestanowitsche
11.5.43 " Stanowitschi
8.6.43 " Beresina-Brod
11.6.43 " Beresina-Uborok
13.6.43 " Beresina-Uborok
14.6.43 " Beresina-Uborok
16.6.43 " Beresina-Uborok
20.7.43 " Osowo
21.7.43 " Osowo
[illegible]
31.7.43 " Nause-Wald
17.8.43 " Szezorse
9.1.44 " Wawiorka

Kampf-tage	Tag	Ort nach Batls.-Befehl	Bescheinigung d. Komp.-Fhrs.
1.	18.1.43	Mokrady-Selitsche	
2.	29.1.43	Chotajewitsche	
3.	7.3.43	Bobrowo	
4.	7.4.43	Pleschtschenize	
5.	1.5.43	Pohost-Sakowitsche	
6.	3.5.43	Krasnoje-Klinska	
7.	4.5.43	Bobrowo	
8.	5.5.43	Bobrowo-Waldlager	
9.	6.5.43	Klein-Nestanowitsche	
10.	11.5.43	Stanowitsche	
11.	8.6.43	Brod	
12.	11.6.43	Uborok	
13.	13.6.43	Uborok	
14.	14.6.43	Uborok	
15.	16.6.43	Uborok	
16.	20.7.43	Osowo	
17.	21.7.43	Osowo	
18.	27.7.43	Polaszna	

Dienststelle:
Bem.

	R								L							
	8	7	6	5	4	3	2	1	1	2	3	4	5	6	7	8
Oben																
Unten																

Datum: Unterschrift:
Dienststelle:
Bem.

	R								L							
	8	7	6	5	4	3	2	1	1	2	3	4	5	6	7	8
Oben																
Unten																

Datum: Unterschrift:
Dienststelle:
Bem.

21

Bescheinigungen über Änderungen und Ergänzungen

soweit nicht schon auf S. 3 oder 4 des Buches eingetragen.

Die Änderung und die Seite des Buches, auf der sie angebracht wurden, sind anzugeben; Datum, Unterschrift, Dienstgrad, Dienststelle und Dienstsiegel sind unter jeder Bescheinigung anzubringen.

Police Brigade "Siegling"

Soon after launching their summer offensive on 22 June 1944, the Red Army occupied almost all of the General Commissariat of White Ruthenia, making the position of Senior SS and Police Commander "Central Russia and White Ruthenia" redundant. Interestingly, on 28 July 1944 Himmler ordered the command, which had been located in Schröttersburg, East Prussia, since 11 July, disbanded. This was a sign that he realized that there would be no positive turn for Germany in this war—although he found other words when he addressed the district leaders (*Gauleiter*) in Posen several days later!

While the German SS police regiments of the former Senior SS and Police Commander "Central Russia and White Ruthenia" were in action at the front,[42] the foreign police units received orders to assemble in the area east of Warsaw near Serk—Modlin—Nassielsk.

The German collapse in White Russia resulted in chaos, and in order to bring a degree of order to the numerous more or less intact foreign units, at the end of July 1944 an order was issued to combine these troops into a police brigade.

In a matter of days *SS-Sturmbannführer und Major der Schutzpolizei* Siegling, former commander of Police Battalion 57 and last Senior SS and Police Commander "White Ruthenia and Pripyat," formed four rifle battalions, an artillery battalion, a mounted battalion, and a training battalion. A few days later, on 3 August 1944, Himmler mentioned this at the meeting of district leaders in Posen, in his typical agitation against the army:

"A second unit is under the command of a young Obersturmbannführer and Oberstleutnant of the Schutzpolizei Sickling [Siegling, author's note]. He was a Major; I have made him an Oberstleutnant. The man has 2,000 or 3,000 Russians. During the retreat he gathered 9-10,000, all excellently clothed. I asked: from where? He said: the clothing depots were all up front, all we had to do was go there and drive in, the Russians hadn't got there yet but the Germans had already left, and a few times a bottle of schnapps was enough for me to keep the administrative people from setting everything on fire, and then we clothed and armed ourselves."

The 1st Regiment under the command of *SS-Hauptsturmführer und Hauptmann der Schutzpolizei* Österreich was formed in Grady from the remnants of Police Battalions 57, 60, and 61, plus elements of White Ruthenian Home Defense Battalion 34.

The 2nd Regiment under the command of *SS-Hauptsturmführer und Hauptmann der Schutzpolizei* Gautz was formed in Stawics from the remnants of Police Battalions 62, 63, and 64.

The 3rd Regiment under *SS-Hauptsturmführer und Hauptmann der Schutzpolizei* Mocha was formed in Lida Czartoria from the remnants of Police Battalions 65, 66, and 67, plus personnel from various former police region garrison headquarters.

The 4th Regiment under the command of *SS-Hauptsturmführer und Hauptmann der Schutzpolizei* Schmidt was formed in Snessne by combining the remnants of

White Ruthenian Home Defense Battalions 23 and 34, plus the personnel of various former police region garrison headquarters.

The Artillery Battalion was formed from Police Artillery Battalion 56 in Suliny.

The Mounted Battalion was also formed in Suliny from the former Cossack Mounted Battalion 68.

Just four weeks later, on 31 July 1944, Police Brigade "Siegling" was renamed *30. Waffen-Grenadier-Division der Waffen-SS ((russische) Nr. 2)*.

White Ruthenian Home Defense

On 23 February 1944, as part of the general mobilization in the eastern areas, *SS-Gruppenführer und Generalleutnant der Polizei von Gottberg*, the Senior SS and Police Commander "Central Russia and White Ruthenia," ordered the formation of the White Ruthenia Home Defense to fight bolshevism.

The formation was to be undertaken step by step in all parts of the General Commissariat of White Ruthenia, except for the areas of the SS and Police Commander "Pripyat" (*SS-Sturmbannführer und Major der Schutzpolizei* Siegling) and the Lida war zone. Likewise, there was to be no recruiting in the already-established or planned defense villages or in several other *rayons*.

Proclaimed on 21 December 1943, the White Ruthenian central council initially mobilized all former officers up to age class 57 and all former non-commissioned officers up to age 55. Mustering was carried out in each district by a committee consisting of two doctors and a member of the White Ruthenian central council. While some of the officers and NCOs were sent to Minsk for a three-week training course, receiving general military and weapons training from *Hauptmann der Schutzpolizei* Schneider—a member of the Senior SS and Police Command "Central Russia and White Ruthenia"—the rest immediately set about mobilizing the enlisted men. These were to be recruited from the year classes 1908 to 1917 (27 to 36 years) and 1921 to 1924 (20 to 23 years).

The year classes 1925, 1926, and 1927 (17 to 19 years) were called into the White Ruthenian Youth. With the German retreat from White Russia, by order of *Generalkommissar* von Gottberg the White Ruthenian and Russian youth organizations were taken charge of by Hitler Youth *Oberbannführer* Schulz. On 25 March 1944 an agreement was reached between the Reich Youth Leader and the State Ministry for the Occupied Eastern Areas and SS Command, by which young volunteers could be recruited for military service. Until 20 September 1944, 1,383 Russian and 2,354 White Ruthenian so-called "SS auxiliaries" were employed as anti-aircraft auxiliaries.

The year classes 1918-1920 (24 to 26 years) were taken into the police units.

The order that members of the White Ruthenian Home Defense not be issued uniforms, wearing armbands over civilian clothing to identify them as combatants, is typical of the situation at that time and displays parallels to the *Volkssturm* later raised in Germany. All members of the White Ruthenian Home Defense had to take the following oath:

"As a member of the White Ruthenian Home Defense, I swear before almighty God and military honor to faithfully serve the White Ruthenian people and to honestly carry out all orders from my superiors.

I swear not to lay down my weapons at the side of the German soldier until peace has returned to our towns and cities, until the last enemy on our soil has been destroyed.

I swear that I would rather die as a hero than allow my wife and children, parents and brothers and sisters, and the entire White Ruthenian people to again fall under the yoke and mistreatment of bolshevism.

Should I break this oath out of my own weakness or malice, God will punish me with the disgraceful death of the traitor to his people and homeland."

When the Germans retreated from White Ruthenia, those who had collaborated with them were evacuated to the area on the Narev and employed in the construction of fortifications. *Major* Müller—appointed Commissar of Refugees by the Reich Minister for the Occupied Eastern Areas—had only an advisory function to the Reich Defense commissars; however, he was to see to it that the special groups of interest to Germany were kept together and treated uniformly.

The planned formation of 60 home defense battalions with a total strength of 30,000 men was not realized. In fact, in the area of Army Group Center only single battalions were formed, most of which were then disbanded in September 1944. While two battalions were employed in Army Group North's area in East Prussia in 1944-45, the members of the remaining home defense battalions were employed as auxiliaries or transferred to the *30. Waffen-Grenadier-Division der SS (russische Nr. 2)*. Established were:

White Ruthenian Home Defense Pioneer Battalion 1 (May 1944, 3 companies)

White Ruthenian Home Defense Pioneer Battalion 2 (June 1944, 3 companies)

White Ruthenian Home Defense Pioneer Battalion 7 (June 1944, 3 companies)

White Ruthenian Home Defense Pioneer Battalion 9 (July 1944, with 4th Army/East Prussia 1944-45)

White Ruthenian Home Defense Pioneer Battalion 11 (July 1944, with Army Group North in 1945)

White Ruthenian Home Defense Battalion 23 (Armenians and Poles in Byten)

White Ruthenian Home Defense Battalion 34 (Stolpce)

The White Ruthenian Home Defense Pioneer Battalions 3-6, 8, 10, 12, and 13 were not established, nor were battalions 14-22, 23-33, and 35-60.

30. Waffen-Grenadier-Division der SS (russische Nr. 2)

When, following the failed assassination attempt on 20 July 1944, Hitler named the *Reichsführer-SS* commander of the Replacement Army, Himmler tackled his new job with élan. In his search for immediately-employable units, he discovered Police Brigade Siegling and proposed to Hitler that it form the basis of a division of the *Waffen-SS*. Hitler gave his approval, and on 31 July 1944 the *Reichsführer-SS* ordered the unit transferred from the uniformed regular police to the *Waffen-SS*. On 18 August 1944, SS Command Central announced:[43]

"By order of the Reichsführer-SS, effective 1/8/44 Police Brigade Siegling, consisting of units and formations made up of Ukrainian, Russian and White Ruthenian volunteers, is transferred with all personnel and materiel to the Waffen-SS. Police Brigade Siegling is renamed and reorganized as

30. Waffen-Grenadier-Division der SS (russische Nr. 2).

Named to command the 30. Waffen-Grenadier-Division der SS (russische Nr. 2) is SS-Obersturmbannführer Siegling."

The oath for the foreign soldiers read:

"I swear to God this sacred oath, that in the struggle against the bolshevist enemies of my homeland I will render unconditional obedience to the Supreme Commander of the German Armed Forces, Adolf Hitler, and as a brave soldier will be ready to lay down my life at any time for this oath."

Although the formation order spoke of Ukrainian, Russian, and White Ruthenian volunteers, the suffix read "Russian No. 2." This shows that in designating its foreign units, the SS Command Central—for propaganda purposes—in fact gave little consideration to their ethnic makeup.[44] In the case of the *30. Waffen-Grenadier-Division der SS (russische Nr. 2)*, this is verified by a report by the 3rd Battalion of the 4th Regiment. According to it, of the unit's 583 men there were:

447 White Ruthenians
53 Russians
15 Ukrainians
65 Poles
3 Tartars

Interestingly, the ethnic makeup of the battalion was roughly equivalent to that of White Ruthenia.[45]

On 3 August 1944, *SS-Hauptsturmführer* Deutschbein, the chief of operations, announced that the foreign members of the division now had to salute with the "German salute" just like the Germans—since 20 July 1944.

As well, the rank designations of the former police units and policemen were changed to those of the *Waffen-SS*.

Anwärter/Schutzmann	*SS-Grenadier/Waffen-Grenadier*
Unterwachtmeister/Unterkorporal	*SS-Sturmmann/Waffen-Sturmman*
Rottwachtmeister/Vizekorporal	*SS-Rottenführer/Waffen-Rottenführer*
Wachtmeister46	*SS-Unterscharführer*
Oberwachtmeister/Korporal	*SS-Scharführer/Waffen-Scharführer*
Zugwachtmeister/Vizefeldwebel	*SS-Oberscharführer/Waffen-Oscha.*
Hauptwachtmeister/Kompaniefeldwebel	*SS-Hauptscharführer/Waffen-Hscha.*
Meister	*SS-Sturmscharführer*

As shortages of heavy weapons and equipment and the specialist personnel needed to operate them, as well as the absence of individual and unit training made it impossible to establish an operational frontline division, it was decided to employ the division in the anti-partisan role, in keeping with its previous role. On 4 August 1944 the war diary of the Commander-in-Chief West recorded the planned deployment of the two Russian SS Waffen Grenadier divisions:

"*Order for transfer of the 29. and 30. Waffen-Grenadier-Division der SS (russische Nr. 1 und 2) into the OB West's area for anti-terrorist operations (Divisions presently engaged in suppressing the Warsaw uprising*[47]*; strength 6-7,000 and 9,000 men respectively). Further orders from chief intelligence officer.*"

The transfer was ordered because the feared unreliability was manifesting itself. On 5 August 1944 the 12th Company of the 4th Regiment reported:

"*After the objective of the day was reached on 5/8/44 it was discovered that the following foreign Waffen-Grenadiers of the former police station in Lohischyn had left their unit without permission:*

1. Andreas Chonitsch
2. Andreas Lewoschyk
3. Vladimir Syzewitsch
4. Paul Bonzewitsch
5. Simon Zawazki

The grenadiers left without weapons in White Ruthenian police uniforms."

More serious, however, was the fact that foreign officers, often of Polish heritage, made contact with the Polish Home Army and convinced their soldiers to join it. The *Wehrmacht* garrison post in Warsaw submitted one report documenting this:

"*At dusk on 7/8 a division train headquarters was attacked by about 300 men in Polish uniforms*[48] *[armed] with several machine-guns and hand grenades about 1.5 km north of the Babice (12 km west of Warsaw) to Zaborow (22 km west of Warsaw). Women and children from the village were forced to advance in front of them. In the ensuing lengthy battle several of the enemy were killed, as was one of our own men.*

After the incident was reported the group was stopped by police in White Ruthenia and immediately committed against Soviet bandits. NCOs and men were mostly White Ruthenian, the officers all Polish, who spoke Polish in conversing with the men. The men were kept in the dark as to intentions and objectives.

Formation (as a police battalion) probably took place near Baranowicze toward mid-June 1944. On 29/6 the formed battalion began falling back to the west from Minsk to Stolpce, Slonim, Wolkowysk and Bialystok, always together with the German armed forces, field police and police. The battalion halted in Neuhof near Modlin for about a week and on 1/8—for the first time without accompanying German units—pulled back into the wooded area west of Lipkow (13 km NW Warsaw). On 5/8 quarters were occupied in blockhouses at the south end of the forest. Receipt of rations and equipment from German stores ceased with the withdrawal from Neuhof.

The battalion had a strength of 600 men in three companies, 1 cavalry troop and 1 machine-gun platoon. Company train had 30 horses, 15 vehicles, including 3 ammunition trucks.

Armament of each company (apart from Russian carbines, hand grenades and several SMGs) 3 light Russian machine-guns, 2 heavy Russian machine-guns. The machine-gun platoon was equipped entirely with Russian machine-guns, roughly 6 heavy machine-guns.

Uniforms Polish, underwear and equipment German.

A number of Polish bandits from the Las Lisia Gora forest area took part in the attack. Officers of the Polish—White Ruthenian battalion made contact and negotiated with the Polish bandits. The Polish battalion's separation from German units on 1/8 leads to the conclusion that it was linked to the breakout by the Warsaw rebels. There is the solid impression that the Polish officers are using their White Ruthenian soldiers as tools for the uprising."

To prevent such occurrences in the future, the German command tried to get the scattered foreign units—whose diminishing motivation had become abundantly clear—into the East-Prussian assembly area as quickly as possible. When the future units of the *30. Waffen-Grenadier-Division der SS (russische Nr. 2)* reached the Osterode area on 10 August 1944, the young division commander, *SS-Obersturmbannführer* Siegling, sensing the potential danger emanating from the foreigners, issued the following order:

"*The division has arrived in the temporary quartering area on old German soil. The mission of all officers and NCOs is to turn the men into capable SS soldiers by conducting intensive training in all areas of combat. The human material is good, strong and resilient. They have all lost their homes. Company, battalion, regiment will be their new home. It is up to us Germans to determine what form this new home will take.*

To this end it is necessary that we see all the foreigners as equal comrades, as the reverse is to be. Calling the foreigners bandits, Bolsheviks, etc—as has already happened—or making threats is completely unacceptable. We have no need to do that. A soldier who fails to carry out an order will be brought before a court martial and is impossible as a soldier in the unit. Anyone who must resort to blows or swearing to have his orders carried out is no NCO.

Let everyone remember that our foreigners will be fighting at our side in the foreseeable future. We will then have the most loyal comrades if we succeed in drawing and binding the foreigners to us, in awakening and nurturing their pride and offering them proof that they are our equals, not just externally in the uniform, but internally as well.

The doctors will be examining the foreigners to quickly identify those who are not medically fit to remain with the unit.

The battalion medics will assist the regimental medical officer. Lists of the unfit are to be submitted immediately by the battalions. The lists are also to include those foreigners who are unfit to belong to the unit for other reasons.[49] *[...]*

The units are to submit continuous reports on behavior in the quartering area. The unit leaders are to convey in a suitable manner to residents living in the quartering area that they are to immediately report any excesses, even of a minor nature, to the unit leaders."

These instructions are interesting in a number of ways. On the one hand they demonstrate the attitude of the 32-year-old division commander, and on the other reveal the problems created by the hasty formation of the division. As subsequent events would reveal, within the unit there were about 3,000 foreign soldiers with no motivation to continue in German service! These were nationalities, some of which had been evacuated by Germany from other areas of the Soviet Union to White Ruthenia and integrated into the White Ruthenian home defense or police battalions.

The insults and the corporal punishments handed out by the overage German core personnel (some over 45 years old) demonstrated the helplessness in the face of the situation. One must note that, as a rule, the German officers and NCOs had already served in the police battalions and were familiar with the mentality of the foreigners. While assisting with the harvest in mid-August 1944, many members of the division deserted. About 300 men were subsequently mustered out and remaining in Rosenberg as workers.

Anti-Terrorist Operations in France

On 15 August 1944 the American VI Corps and the French II Corps of the U.S. 7th Army landed in southern France. Positioned there was the German 19th Army (Army Group G), the bulk of which consisted of locally-based reserve divisions and several exhausted units from the Eastern and Invasion Fronts. To prevent the predictable loss of the German troops to an Allied pincer movement, the next day Hitler authorized the evacuation of southern and southwestern France.

Two days later *Generalfeldmarschall* Model was named Commander-in-Chief West. He immediately asked Hitler for three more infantry divisions to ensure the 19th Army's retreat. French irregulars,[50] in particular, posed a threat to the retreating German forces. Not only were they destroying important objects (supply and fuel dumps, as well as roads and rail lines), with increasing frequency they were also attacking German troops in the rear.

Faced with this situation, Himmler, as commander of the Reserve Army, ordered the immediate transfer of the *30. Waffen-Grenadier-Division der SS (russische Nr. 2)* to France. The members of the division exchanged their black *Schutzmannschaft* clothing (mainly Polish, Lithuanian, or Latvian uniforms dyed black) for green police uniforms and were transported by rail via Deutsch-Eylau – Thorn – Hohensalza – Halle – Worms – Hanau – Frankfurt – Strassburg into the Belfort—Besançon—Dole area. The division commander issued the following order for this transport:

"*Entraining officers to establish contact with Reichsbahn on a timely basis. The prescribed entraining time must be adhered to, any delay due to late arrival is unacceptable. The forces and vehicles coming for entraining are to be at the approach to the loading ramp 1 hour before the arrival of the train. (...)*

The men's luggage is to be stowed first, in order to allow loading of hay and oats to begin as quickly as possible. Eight horses plus one bale of hay, straw and oats must be accommodated in each covered goods wagon. The units are to see to the procurement of flanking posts (length 2.4 m). Wire approximately 20 cm long is to be attached to the ends.

Panye wagons are to be loaded if possible. A flatcar should be loaded with 10 panye wagons. Eight heavy MGs are to be placed on two L-cars (4 heavy MGs per car) for air defense. 3 heavy MGs are to be placed in position ready to fire. 1 heavy MG in reserve. A German team leader is to be selected for each gun team.

During stops no one is to leave the train without orders.

The roofs of enclosed freight cars are not to be occupied. (Danger from overpasses.)

The throwing of remnants or fixed objects from moving cars is strictly forbidden.

At stations the toilet facilities are to be used.

The utmost caution is to be used when crossing tracks. Everyone is to look left and right to ensure that the tracks to be crossed are free and that there are no approaching trains.

Companies are to take on food and fodder for 10 days. Distribution times to be announced.

There is no need to brew coffee, as this will be provided by the NSV at the station."

On 22 August 1944 the war diary of the Commander-in-Chief West reported that 18 transport trains carrying the *30. Waffen-Grenadier-Regiment (russische Nr. 2)* had left the Reich and that 11 had already detrained in Vesoul.[51] The *Wehrmacht* Operations Staff described the importance of the anti-terrorist effort to the withdrawal of the German troops deployed in southern France:

"*There is growing concern about the LXIV Army Corps (Biscay front) and the 19th Army (southern front), as their withdrawal is proceeding slowly and is facing a growing threat from terrorists. The question is, will they be able to reach the line of security in time? The CIC West is urging that the movements be accelerated.*"

This strong partisan activity[52] in the 19th Army's rear resulted in the first elements of the division going into action on 24 August 1944. Army Group G's war diary recorded:[53]

"*Bandit activity on the Rhone roads south of Lyon. Road commanders deployed. Clearance fighting in progress. Traffic north of Lyon trouble free and without stoppages. Security details to be posted after arrival of forces. The 30. SS-Grenadier-Regiment is to be used to clear the Monte de Maconnais area and the Moroz—Lons le Sarnier—Dole—Gray—Besançon—Pontarlier area.*"

Planned area of operations of the 30. Waffen-Grenadier-Division der SS (russische Nr. 2) for anti-terrorist operations.

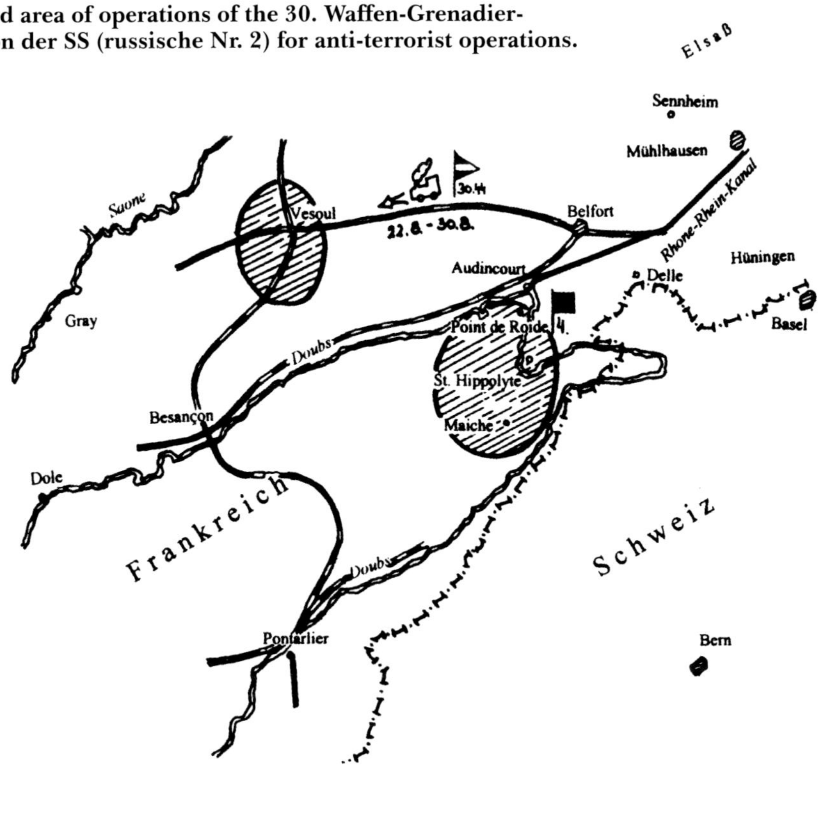

The Gray—Dole—Pontarlier—Besançon area encompassed more than 2,000 km,[2] and thus the order was a totally unrealistic one for the *30. Waffen-Grenadier-Regiment (russische Nr. 2)*. Two days later the Commander-in-Chief West informed Army Group G that Himmler, displaying justified concern, had essentially released the division only for anti-partisan operations:[54]

"By order of the Reichsführer-SS and commander of the Replacement Army, the 30. Panzer-Grenadier-Regiment is attached to the military commander of France for anti-bandit operations only.

Other employment in an emergency as per order to CIC West, Ops Chief War Diary No. 7311/44 Secret of 24/8, but with the reminder that reliability in combat against 'Allies' not assured."

While half the division was still on trains en route to France, the first battalions to see action and not under the control of the division commander caused a furor. On 27 August 1944 the 2nd Battalions of the 1st and 2nd Regiments murdered their German core personnel and defected to the *Résistance*. The next day large elements of the 4th Regiment, deployed against French rebels in the Pont de Roide—St. Hippolyte—Maiche area, deserted to Switzerland. On 28 August 1944 *Generalfeldmarschall* Model reported to SS Central Command:[55]

"30. SS-Panzer-Grenadier-Division deserting to the bandits by battalions, killing German officers, completely unreliable. Division is being disarmed. Immediate return to the Reich for labor duty necessary."

What many had long feared had happened—the foreign divisions had become a serious potential source of trouble. This was in part due to the fact that the men had sworn an oath only to fight against bolshevism and not against the western allies.

In any event, during the course of the day division commander *SS-Obersturmbannführer* Siegling succeeded in regaining control of his units. By that evening the Commander-in-Chief West's war diary was already reporting that the *30. Waffen-Grenadier-Regiment (russische Nr. 2)* was again reliable:

"Immediately available to secure and receive the still-retreating elements of Army Group G are:

a) 30. Waffen-Grenadier-Regiment (russische Nr. 2) presently detraining in Vesoul — Besançon, by and large reliable.

b) II/Rifle Regiment 199, I/Regional Defense Replacement Battalion 7 deployed in the Troyes area,

III/Rifle Regiment 199, East Battalion 615, deployed in the Avallon — Auxerre area, East Battalion 654 deployed northeast of Nevers

I/Rifle Regiment 199 and III/Rifle Regiment 198 deployed Nevers – Le Creuzot area

I/Rifle Regiment 198 deployed Besançon area."

The success of the division commander's rapid action is also confirmed by the war diary of the operations officer of the commander of volunteer units attached to the Commander-in-Chief West on 4 September 1944:

"Again contact with the Commander-in-Chief West. For the first time reports on the 30. SS-Division Siegling, which is made up of Russians and which was committed for the first time a few days ago near Belfort. Held for three days, then became caught up in the general flow of the retreat."

And on 6 September 1944:

"The SS division, until now completely unknown to us, is a unit made up of White Ruthenians, officer corps from White Ruthenian youth. Inadequately armed. Willingness to serve astonishing in view of the general collapse."

The inadequate German core personnel were also partly responsible for the incidents—as earlier in the departure of the White Ruthenians. It was also found that units made up largely of Poles were less reliable. On 29 August 1944, for example, the 4th Regiment reported on the deserters:

"As all of the deserters spoke only Polish when they were alone, it is assumed that they were Polish nationals even though they have always passed themselves off as White Russians."

Reorganization of the Division

On 30 August 1944, with the detraining of all 31 transport trains, the transfer of the division from East Prussia to France was complete. That same day, however, it was ordered out of the Point de Roide area to Alsace for reorganization in Defense District V.

SS-Obersturmbannführer Siegling removed all "*unusable and unreliable elements*" from his division, and from them assembled two construction regiments with a total strength of 37 officers and 2,331 other ranks. These unarmed personnel were initially attached to Transport Control Headquarters Karlsruhe and then assigned to expand the Westwall.[56] Formed were:

Construction Regiment 1 consisting of 14 foreign officers and 512 men of the 4th Regiment and 4 foreign officers and 664 men of the 3rd Regiment.

Construction Regiment 2 consisting of 19 foreign officers and 1,155 men of the 1st and 2nd Regiments and the Reconnaissance Regiment.

The division's long overdue reorganization was carried out using the approximately 6,200 remaining men (home base: Eutingen/Wurttemberg). As per division order No. 4 of 14 September 1944 the unit was to be established with two regiments each of three battalions. The unit now consisted of:

Division Headquarters (base: Marckolsheim)

Regiment 1 – later Waffen-Grenadier-Regiment der SS 75 – (base: Mussig) with:
- I Battalion (remains of former 1st Regiment)
- II Battalion (remains of former 2nd Regiment)
- III Battalion (newly-created "Muravyev Battalion"[57])
  - Base: Streitkopf water training grounds

Regiment 2[58] – later Waffen-Grenadier-Regiment der SS 76 – (base: Saasenheim) with:
- I Battalion (remains of former 3rd Regiment)
- II Battalion (remains of former 4th Regiment)
- III Battalion (newly-attached East Battalion 654[59]; base: Bootzheim)

- Reconnaissance Battalion (base: Mackenheim) with:
  - three cavalry troops (former Cossack Cavalry Battalion 68)
- Panzer-Grenadier Battalion (base: Elsenheim) with:
  - one panzer-grenadier and one armored patrol company
- Artillery Battalion (base: Hessenheim) with:
  - two batteries of 122-mm field howitzers and one rocket battery

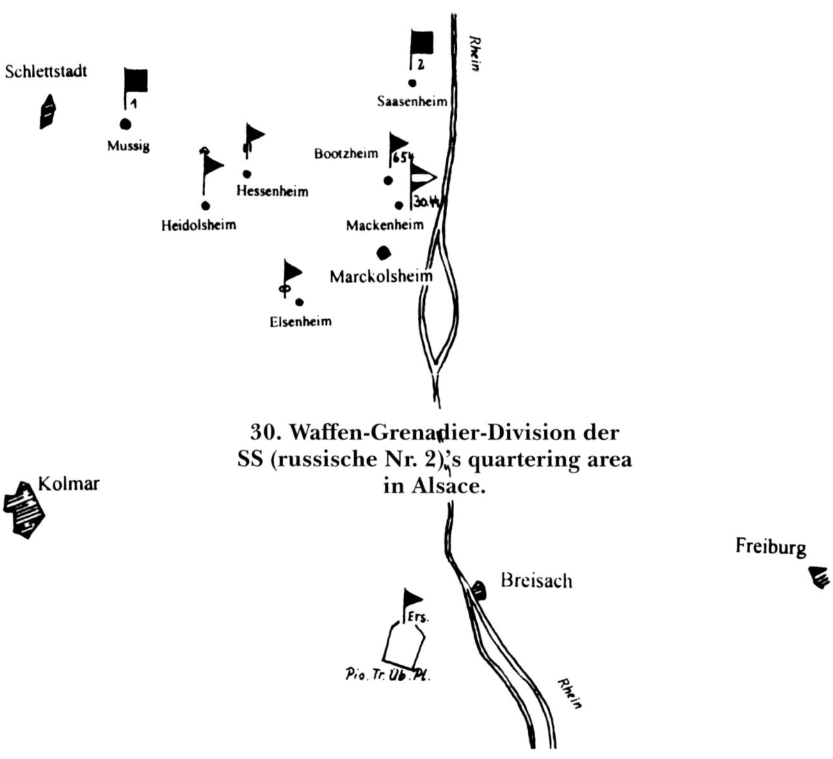

30. Waffen-Grenadier-Division der SS (russische Nr. 2)'s quartering area in Alsace.

Pioneer Company (base: Heidolsheim)
Mixed Signals Company (base: Mackolsheim)
Field Replacement Battalion (base: Breisach pioneer training grounds) with:
three rifle companies and one heavy company
Supply Services (base: Mackolsheim)

It is interesting that the division had almost no heavy weapons. Instead of an artillery regiment with four battalions it had just a single artillery battalion. There was no anti-tank battalion at all. This fact was to have extremely negative consequences when the division went into action.

Coincident with the reorganization, the division commander ordered that the customary forms of address like *officer* or *administration official* be replaced by *leader (Führer)* or *administration leader*, respectively.

The following extracts from the war diary of a battalion of the 2nd Regiment [*Waffen-Grenadier-Regiment der SS 76 (russische Nr. 5)*] are offered to provide an insight into the daily routine:

"*21 September 1944*

A division order telling the battalion that it was to occupy quarters in Jobsheim arrived late. Preparations were made for departure. Morale is generally good, because bivouacking in tents in bad weather is coming to an end.

22 September 1944

Battalion loaded onto panye wagons and departure for Jobsheim. Quarters subsequently set up in empty flats, barns and halls.

26 September 1944

Division runner brought an alert order with the following content:

"According to information from the commanding general of the rear area, the dropping of enemy paratroops is to be expected. The units are to come to alert status, signed Siegling."

The company commanders, weapons technicians and functionaries were immediately ordered to a situation briefing and appropriate measures were taken. [...] The company commanders and some NCOs were briefed on the Panzerfaust and Panzerschreck.

30 September 1944

Combat firing in the presence of the division commander (platoon attack 400 meters). The division commander subsequently praised the men's spirit. The uniformity of dress and the design and layout of the exercise also received praise. The men were promised five additional cigarettes as a gift from the division commander, which caused much celebration.

3 October 1944

Attack exercise in battalion formation. Afterwards the division commander arrived to present two grenadiers with the Bravery and Merit Decoration for Members of the Eastern Peoples in Bronze. At the same time these men were each presented with a pocket watch and a bottle of schnapps for their skilled capture of two enemy agents.

5 October 1944

Speech by Rittmeister Gravenhorst concerning the political situation and new weapons as well as the events of 20 July in the town hall meeting room. All German officers, NCOs and German-speaking foreigners attended. The affair ended with an affirmation of loyalty to the Führer and people, when the battalion commander addressed the men with the closing words.

7 October 1944

The battalion commander and a company commander took part in a regimental exercise as guests of the 1st Regiment. In the afternoon two films were shown. The men were visibly pleased. Shown were a newsreel and the film "Tonelli".

15 October 1944

Division band played in the Wittishain market square. Free time presentations at the same time. Each company sent a group of singers to Wittishain; the 12th Company's was acknowledged as the best. The population played an active part in the show.

17 October 1944

Regimental exercise. Bivouac, advance under difficult conditions. Reconnaissance by cavalry troop, assault operation against bunkers, attack after cursory preparations. Division commander in attendance."

On 19 October 1944 the SS Central Command Office ordered the SS unit reorganized into a new-style 1944 infantry division. The two grenadier regiments were each reduced to two battalions and a third regiment formed. As well, the grenadier regiments were for the first time issued the consecutive numbers 75 to 77 (Russian numbers 4 to 6) of the *Waffen-SS*.

After the German troops had lost a not inconsiderable quantity of materiel in the retreat from southern France, on 24 October 1944 the leadership remembered the still-armed *30. Waffen-Grenadier-Regiment (russische Nr. 2)*. Discussions followed between Army Group G and Defense District Command V:

"*In response to an inquiry by the army group operations chief about the 30. SS-Grenadier-Division, which several weeks ago had several of its battalions taken out of action for mutiny and sent to Defense District V, Oberst Adam reported that the bulk of the division was situated west of the Rhine in the Markolsheim area (north of Kolmar). No orders have yet been issued concerning the division. Army Group operations chief discussed the problem of disbanding the division and raising construction battalions. The army group would claim the surrendered weapons for itself. [...] Concerning the 30. SS-Grenadier-Division the commanding officer made reference to the subordination of this division to the commander of the Waffen-SS. A request is to be made to the Commander-in-Chief West to attach the division to the army group, along with a request to release weapons and equipment to reequip divisions of Headquarters, 19th Army.*"

Ignoring the looming threat of disbandment, on 27 October 1944 *SS-Obersturmbannführer* Siegling ordered a division exercise which was to simulate the formation of a bridgehead on the Rhine. Some elements of the division covered a distance of more than 50 kilometers.

Division commander SS-Obersturmbannführer Siegling decorates four Russian Waffen-grenadiers with the Medal of Bravery for Members of the Eastern Peoples.

Action in the Burgundian Gate

On 14 November 1944 French troops under General De Lattre de Tassigny launched a major attack in the Burgundian Gate. The French 1st Armored and 9th Colonial Divisions broke through the weak German front close to the Swiss border. When the French units reached the Mömpelgard area, near Belfort, three days later, *SS-Obersturmbannführer* Siegling offered to commit his *30. Waffen-Grenadier-Regiment (russische Nr. 2)*. Concerning this, Army Group G's war diary recorded on 18 November 1944:

"Commander Headquarters, 19th Army telephoned the army group commander and reported that the commander of the 30. SS-Waffen-Grenadier-Division has offered to commit the 3 regiments and 1 infantry battalion of his division, which is in Kolmar, in response to the armored breakthrough toward Delle.

Army group commander informed the commander of Headquarters, 19th Army of the army group commander-in-chief's decision to reject a combat role for the division, which was taken out of action for mutiny. Only the division's artillery battalion is to be employed in the Belfort area.

Commander-in-chief Headquarters, 19th Army reported that he intends to use the 30. SS-Waffen-Grenadier-Regiment to establish a deep blocking line. Envisaged is the establishment of a strongpoint-style line of security between the Rhine-Rhone Canal and the Swiss border. He requests approval for use of the division in this manner."

Late in the evening Army Group G high command sent a telex to Headquarters, 19th Army:

"The army releases the 30th SS Volunteer Division for action in the Larg Position, to prevent a breakthrough by enemy attack spearheads to the northeast. The division is to be brought in by the army.

198th Infantry Division is to be moved quickly to the army's left wing for a counterattack to restore the situation near Delle and regain the former main line of resistance."

The dramatic development of the situation in the Belfort area, which saw the enemy take Delle, and the subsequent decision to alert the *30. Waffen-Grenadier-Regiment (russische Nr. 2)* were clearly recorded in the 19th Army's war diary entry for 18 November 1944:

"At 1150 hours Corps Headquarters Belfort reported that the corps has lost control in the southern sector. Combat strengths and fighting value of our own units must still be rated quite low. Commander army headquarters subsequently recommended that the corps' right wing absolutely not be weakened further, as the decision as to whether Belfort can be held or not will be made today. IV Luftwaffe Field Corps has received orders to pull out the 198th Infantry Division, which the army group has released for use by Corps Headquarters Belfort, today while it is dark. The first battle groups are to be sent as quickly as possible to Belfort this night, ignoring any concerns or arguments by the division. A request is being made to the army group to immediately release the 30. SS-Waffen-Division with 3 regiments each of 2

battalions (Russians with German core personnel), with the approval of the Reichsführer-SS, for use in the Belfort area. The division is to occupy and secure the Larg position behind the front to the Swiss border. At 1826 hours the army group issued the advance order to alert the 30. SS-Waffen-Division and at a situation briefing by the army headquarters commander-in-chief authorized the employment of the division with the proviso that it is not sent forward into battle on account of its foreign makeup."

On 19 November 1944 the first French troops reached the Rhine, whereupon the *Reichsführer-SS* authorized the employment of the division:[61]

"According to information from the OKW, the Reichsführer-SS agrees to the employment of the 30. SS-Grenadier-Division (r.) with the proviso that it is used as a security force in the Altkirch blocking line.

With the availability of transport space, however, the division must be transported back to the Reich."

The passage specifying that the division be withdrawn from the front as soon as possible and sent to Germany shows the absence of trust that the German command had in the unit.

While during the course of 20 November 1944 the enemy forced his way into Mülhausen and established bridgeheads across the Rhone-Rhine Canal near Bretagne and Montreux Chateau, the grenadier regiments of the 198th Infantry Division launched an attack from the assembly area south of Dammerkirch south in the direction of the Swiss border with the objective of severing the supply lines of the enemy elements that had broken through.

The *30. Waffen-Grenadier-Regiment der SS (russische Nr. 2)* was sent to the LXIII Army Corps for use in the Larg position and took over the positions of the 198th Infantry Division. *Waffen-Grenadier-Regiment der SS 76 (russische Nr. 5)* occupied the line Dammerkirch – Altkirch – Hirtzbach. *Waffen-Grenadier-Regiment der SS 75 (russische Nr. 4)* was positioned along the Rhine-Rhone Canal between Montreux Chateau and Wolfersdorf. By express order of *Generalfeldmarschall* Model, however, it was expressly forbidden that it be used offensively.

Nevertheless *Waffen-Grenadier-Regiment der SS 76* was committed to a limited advance from the Altkirch – Hirtzbach area through Hirsingen – Largitzen toward Friesen – Überstrass. This resulted in fierce street fighting in Hirsingen and Largitzen. SS Reconnaissance Battalion 30 advanced along the Ill toward Waldighofen.

While on 21 November the 198th Infantry Division advanced through Chavanatte and reached the wooded area south of the Grosne – Suarce road, the *30. Waffen-Grenadier-Regiment (russische Nr. 2)* was counterattacked by the French 1st Armored Division and driven back to the line Hindlingen – Hirtzbach.

On that day the high command of Army Group G ordered an assault force to halt enemy supply traffic in the area south and southeast of Mülhausen. It was to consist of 5 to 10 men armed with *Panzerfaust* anti-tank weapons and pressure mines. The 198th Infantry Division and the *30. Waffen-Grenadier-Regiment (russische Nr. 2)* were each supposed to deploy two such assault teams daily in the Courtelevant – Ferette – Muespach – Altkirch area, which covered approximately 200 km^2!

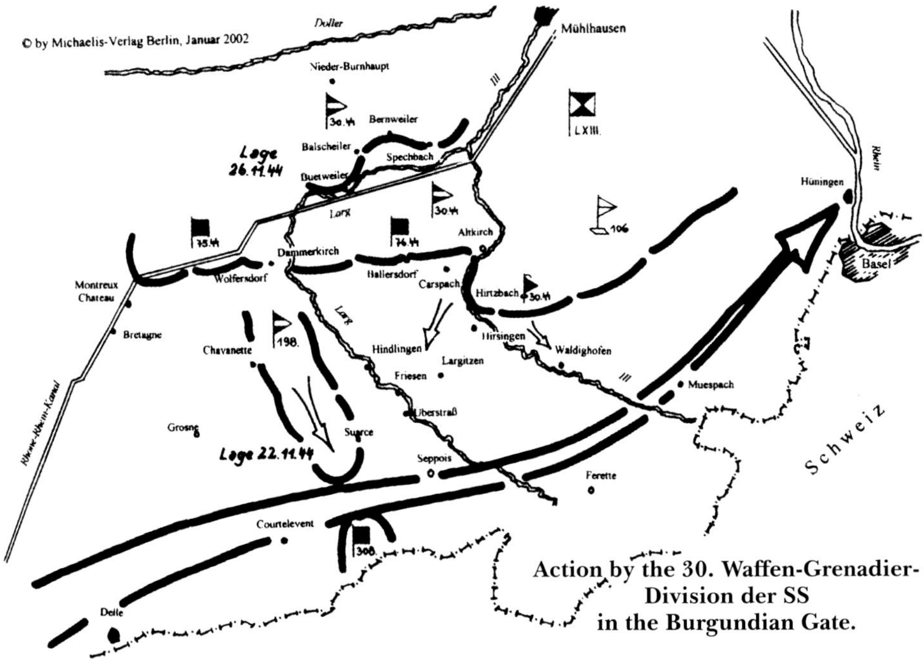

Action by the 30. Waffen-Grenadier-Division der SS in the Burgundian Gate.

After the 198th Infantry Division had reached its objective and Grenadier Regiment 308 had taken the area to the Swiss border, the conditions for the destruction of the encircled enemy forces had been achieved. On 21 November 1944 the 198th Infantry Division was instructed to immediately move east and take Sappois.

In the area west of Altkirch *General der Artillerie* Loch (Senior Commander Eifel) put together a force which was to support the 198th Infantry Division's attack from the northeast. This consisted of:

30. Waffen-Grenadier-Regiment (russische Nr. 2)
Fast Unit Defense District V
Heavy Panzerjäger Battalion 654
Panzer Brigade 106
Assault Gun Brigade 200
scratch units between Altkirch and the Rhine

The attack began on 22 November 1944 from all sectors of the encirclement front with all available forces.

On the first day of the attack the soldiers of the LXIII Army Corps knocked out 41 tanks of the French 1st Armored Division. Of these, six were destroyed by members of the *30. Waffen-Grenadier-Regiment (russische Nr. 2)*. The war diary of the Commander-in-Chief West recorded:

"The 30. SS-Waffen-Grenadier-Regiment (russische Nr. 2) – commander SS-Obersturmbannführer Siegling – has distinguished itself in the fighting in the Burgundian Gate through its bravery and steadfastness. It repeatedly repulsed fierce enemy attacks, destroying 6 enemy tanks.

A request has been made to name [the division] in the supplements to the Wehrmacht communiqué."

This never came to be, however!

The division's success was all the more astonishing, as it was essentially armed with carbines, several machine-guns, and *Panzerfaust* close-range anti-tank weapons. Its only heavy weapons were five 122-mm guns of the artillery battalion.

On 23 November 1944 the French troops recovered from the shock of the unexpected counterattack and began hitting back hard. They succeeded in severing the 198th Infantry Division's wedge to the Swiss border between Courtelevant and Seppois. The French also drove the *30. Waffen-Grenadier-Regiment (russische Nr. 2)* back in several places. Fierce artillery and tank fire caused the latter's fighting power to sink rapidly.

By 24 November, when the surviving elements of Grenadier Regiment 308 crossed the Swiss border into internment,[62] the Russian soldiers had already been forced back to their starting positions. The 19th Army's front now ran in the line Rhine – northeast Erstein – Erstein – Hohwald – Markirch – Vosges crest position to east of Ballon d'Alsace – Dollern – Masevaux – Fontaine – Montreux – Altkirch – Rhine.

The next day the Russian waffen-grenadiers withdrew further to the north into the Spechbach – Bernweiler area. Ignoring the precarious situation, the Commander-in-Chief West ordered a renewed offensive by the 198th Infantry Division. On 26 November 1944 the 19th Army's war diary recorded:

"High Command Eifel to initiate renewed advance to the south to halt enemy troop and supply traffic on the Faverois – Seppois road. The Sturmpanthers moved forward to the south are to take part. The current main line of resistance is to be held on the rest of the front. Squads from Panzerjäger Abteilung 654 are to be readied in the Altenach, Heimsbrunn and Pulversheim areas to intervene immediately against enemy armored thrusts, supporting the front held by the 198th Infantry Division and the 30. Waffen-Grenadier-Regiment (russische Nr. 2) and reinforcing the western and northern fronts of Mühlhausen. The Sturmpanzer will remain corps reserve under their commander and are not to be attached to any division. The assault tanks are to be provided with adequate supporting infantry. Movements by the tank destroyer battalion must be completed by dawn.

At 0236 hours High Command Eifel was advised by telephone that the CIC West has fundamentally rejected any withdrawal of the front on the left wing. Rather the left wing must be sufficiently strengthened to prevent the passage of tanks and supplies. Commander High Command Eifel responded by describing the seriousness of his own situation, especially that of the 30. Waffen-Grenadier-Regiment (russische Nr. 2). When tanks appeared the Russians have fled their positions without firing a shot, and in some cases are fighting against us. If no reinforcements are sent, corps headquarters believes that it will no longer be able to accept responsibility for the front. Despite serious reservations on the part of the division commander, the attack by the 198th Infantry Division will be carried out tonight as ordered."

The panicky behavior of the Russians shows that the German officers no longer had control of their units. The motivation of the foreign soldiers had again reached a low point. The absence of vital anti-tank guns led to a feeling of helplessness. One cannot stop tanks with rifles.

The elements of the 198th Infantry Division which immediately attacked again suffered heavy casualties to enemy infantry fire while still forming up. The battalions, some down to no more than 20 men, were soon forced onto the defensive again. The *30. Waffen-Grenadier-Regiment (russische Nr. 2)* was also involved in fierce defensive fighting. The French troops, especially from Altkirch, advanced on the Russian soldiers, whose steadfastness dropped steadily. The division commander advised corps headquarters of the poor physical condition of his men, who were also suffering as a result of days of bad weather (steady rain). The soldiers were completely soaked, their foxholes filled with water.

On 26 November a 383-man-strong battle group was formed from personnel of SS Supply Regiment 30 and SS Field Replacement Battalion 30. The scratch unit saw action with LXIX Army Corps on the 19th Army's northern front in the Eschenau area.

The next day the troops of LXIII Army Corps withdrew towards the Doller River line. At the same time the Russian soldiers were engaged in fierce defensive fighting for the towns of Buetweiler, Balschweiler and Bernweiler, and tried to halt armored attacks from Balschweiler and Bernweiler in the direction of Niederburnhaupt. When on 28 November the division was withdrawn from the southern front for deployment with LXXXX Army Corps in the Rappoltsweiler area, *SS-Obersturmbannführer* Siegling prevented a further employment of his unit: "*Unit no longer capable of operations, its use will instead mean danger!*"

Siegling did, however, form a second battle group from those men still capable of fighting, and it was sent to LXXXX Army Corps in a replacement role. After turning in its weapons and equipment, the rest of the *30. Waffen-Grenadier-Regiment (russische Nr. 2)* crossed the Rhine at Neuenburg, and on 2 December 1944 arrived at the Münsingen troop training grounds. The two battle groups followed on 7 December. In Münsingen the Russian members of the division were attached to the *600. Infanterie-Division (russische)* and the remaining German and foreign members sent to Grafenwöhr for reorganization.

A former German member recalled the operation in Alsace:

"As an SS-Obersturmführer, in mid-November 1944 I was detached from the administrative officer school in Arolsen to the 30. Waffen-Grenadier-Regiment (russische Nr. 2). Late in the evening I arrived in Markolsheim together with three NCOs, whom I met on the train. Except for a skeleton crew, however, I found no one from headquarters there. We initially took up quarters in private accommodations, but after a display of initiative by an overly-enthusiastic NCO at about 2 o'clock in the morning we were driven to the division assembly area in a rations truck.

We came upon a Russian unit in a wood surrounded by numerous fields. The conditions, which I was able to see in spite of the darkness, gave me cause for concern. Only the Waffen-Untersturmführer, who spoke broken German, and probably three NCOs were armed. These three NCOs were also standing guard. If the Gaullists had appeared they could have nabbed the whole thing easily. A large tent had been set up, in which a few soldiers were squatting around a small stove. Most, however, lay scattered about in the tent, some of them simply on the bare ground! In my opinion many of them were totally drunk—nevertheless, I must give the men their due for their undemanding behavior.

Sleep was out of the question, as it was quite cold and I had nothing with me apart from my coat and a blanket. I was very happy when morning came and the field kitchen handed out coffee and a kind of goulash (!). Surprisingly, the Russian soldiers fell in for morning roll call in a relatively orderly fashion and I was able to take a closer look at them.

The Untersturmführer made a good impression but was unable to tell me how I was supposed to get to headquarters, which was probably in Hagenbach. In the morning weapons were distributed—when questioned by a Russian platoon leader I and a German NCO took over a Czech Type 26 light machine-gun.

At about 1000 hours were alerted and took up defensive positions in the forest against the enemy troops. The grenadiers immediately began digging in and we also sought a good field of fire. Before I saw anything, small arms fire erupted farther in front of us. Then I saw enemy soldiers and opened fire with the machine-gun. I had a good feeling that we would hold our positions until shells suddenly started falling around us and the Russian grenadiers left their positions. During this movement the enemy attacked again and everything became rather confused. The NCO was hit in the face by a fragment and I lost sight of him. Soon afterwards I was also hit by shell fragments, in both legs. Unable to move, I saw my assistant gunner running around in the forest, and I shouted to him that he should take over the machine-gun. He tried to help me, but I kept yelling that he should just take the machine-gun and go into position. His face bloodied, he took the gun and ran off—I didn't see him again. I clenched my teeth and crawled to the rear. Unsure of where I was, I was suddenly hailed by a Russian Waffen-Untersturmführer. He waved to me and I reached him in a small position. He asked if I had any ammunition—I pointed to my PPK pistol and said yes. In the meantime it had become somewhat quieter and I noticed that there were about 6 other men from the platoon there. A short time later the enemy fired at us with automatic weapons; we replied with a few shots. The five bullets in my pistol were quickly expended, and reloading with clammy fingers (cold and wet) took all the longer. When a shell landed right in front of me, everything before my eyes went black and I lost consciousness. I woke up in a field hospital and thank God I was able to stand. In 1948 I was released from a French POW camp as war-disabled."

Formation of the *30. Waffen-Grenadier-Regiment (weißruthenische Nr. 1)*

Following the transfer of about 1,000 Russian members of the division to the 600th Infantry Division at the Münsingen troop training grounds, on 31 December 1944 the *30. Waffen-Grenadier-Regiment (russische Nr. 2)* was disbanded at the Grafenwöhr troop training grounds.[63] SS Supply Regiment 30 received orders to proceed with its more than 100 horse-drawn vehicles to the Neuhammer troop training grounds to join the *25. Waffen-Grenadier-Division der SS "Hunyadi" (ungarische Nr. 1).*

The former Cossack Cavalry Battalion 68 was detached to the *26. Waffen-Grenadier-Division der SS "Hungaria" (ungarische Nr. 2)*, and on 7 January 1945 arrived at the Schieradz troop training grounds. The Cossacks had the job of securing the division's quartering area, which resulted in skirmishes with Polish partisans. One troop formed the Division Security Company. The division's situation was chaotic. On 12 January 1945 the Soviets launched their winter offensive and the Schieradz training grounds quickly became directly threatened. To avoid being overrun by the Soviets, the commander of the *26. Waffen-Grenadier-Division der SS "Hungaria" (ungarische Nr. 2), Waffen-Oberführer* von Pisky, ordered his unit to pull back in the direction of Posen. On 21 January 1945 the division commander, together with his orderly officer *Waffen-Obersturmführer* Kásás and the Cossack troop, became involved in a firefight with advancing Red Army troops and were killed.

Meanwhile, in Grafenwöhr, a *Waffen-Grenadier-Brigade der SS (weißruthenische Nr. 1)* was formed from the remaining German core personnel and White Ruthenian soldiers (especially from the former Police Battalions 60, 64, 65, 66, and 67). About 2,000 men strong, the brigade consisted of:

Waffen-Grenadier-Regiment der SS 75 (weißruthenische Nr. 1)
a reconnaissance troop
an anti-tank company
a field replacement company

In order to deceive enemy intelligence, on 9 March 1945 Himmler ordered the unit renamed the *30. Waffen-Grenadier-Division der SS (weißruthenische Nr. 1).* The unit never saw action; instead, it was disbanded at the beginning of April 1945. The OKW war diary contains the following general comment:

"The formation of non-German divisions was halted at the beginning of April."

Thus ended the history of this second Russian division of the *Waffen-SS*. From the German core personnel *SS-Obersturmbannführer* Siegling formed a police battalion, which was attached to the *38. SS-Grenadier-Division "Niebelungen."*[64] From 21 to 26 April 1945, Police Battalion "Siegling" was deployed near Kehlheim on the Danube (Bad Göging) as the right neighbor of the II./SS-Grenadier-Regiment 95. By way of Landshut and Wasserburg, in May 1945 it reached the area around the Chiemsee and was captured by the Americans.

SS Unit "Drushina"

Following the obvious failure of the Blitzkrieg campaign against the Soviet Union, at the beginning of 1942 Hitler directed Himmler, among others, to step up considerably secret service activity in the USSR. Part of this was the so-called "Zeppelin Action," which was initiated by an order dated 10 March 1942. Its stated purpose was "*To take pressure off the Eastern Front—even if only to a modest extent.*"

The *Reichsführer-SS* tasked the head of Department VI of the Reich Central Security Office, *SS-Brigadeführer* Walter Schellenerg, with carrying out the action. *SS-Obersturmbannführer* Dr. Gräfe—head of section VI C—gave *SS-Sturmbannführer* Dr. Oebsger-Röder the task of selecting and leading the volunteers—all strictly anti-Soviet—to be recruited in the POW camps for sabotage missions behind enemy lines.

As it proved impossible to fully realize[66] the planned insertion of the insurgents in the Russian hinterland, approximately 500 of these volunteers were used to form a special battalion of the SD under the command of the former Soviet Lieutenant-Colonel Radionov. In May 1942 the Radionov Battalion was sent to the Senior SS and Police Commander "Central Russia" in the Nevel area, where it was employed in the anti-partisan role. Together with Police Battalion 57 (Siegling), the battalion formed the "Naumann Group" for special operations.[67]

Even though the Russian volunteers were selected and checked out by the SD (Security Service) in spring 1942, by autumn of that year it also became apparent that they could not be sure of the loyalty of these volunteers. During the night of 24-25 November 1942 63 members of the 1st Company deserted to the partisans near Kolichenko.

From 18 to 27 January 1943 the Radionov Battalion—together with other units, including the SS Special Battalion "Dirlewanger"—took part in "Operation Harvest Festival I." The area to be swept was bordered by: in the north the Cherwen – Minsk road to Kuliki; and in the west the line Kuliki – Rovnopolye (on the Marina – Gorka – Minsk rail line) – Shazk collective farm – Byelaya Luya – road to Slutsk to the outskirts of Slutsk. Also in the south the Slutsk – Stary Dorogi road, in the east the Stary Dorogi – Osipovichi – Marina – Gorka rail line – Marina – Gorka – Cherwen road. The mission order given the men involved was unmistakable:

"*Attack and destroy the bandits. Every bandit, Jew, gypsy and suspected bandit is to be considered the enemy. Special emphasis is to be placed on seizing agricultural products.*"

From 30 January to 15 February 1943 this operation was followed by "Operation Harvest Festival II" in the Minsk – Ivenets to the Slutsk – Brest road. Many farms were burned to the ground, and captured animals and feed were handed over to the district agricultural leader.

From 16 to 26 February 1943 the Russian volunteers took part in "Operation Hornung." Led by *SS-Brigadeführer und Generalmajor der Polizei* von Gottberg, the operation was aimed at the estimated 3,000 to 4,000 partisans in the Morocz –

Milewicze – Lenin – Hryczynowicze – Lugi – Hawrylczyce – Wieliczkowiecze area. They posed a threat to traffic on the Gomel – Luniniece – Brest rail line and caused unrest in the northern part of the Ukraine and the southern part of White Ruthenia. The Radionov Battalion was attached to Battle Group East under the command of *SS-Standartenführer* Anhalt, commanding officer of Police Regiment 2. A total of five battle groups were to strike quickly from their assembly areas and encircle and destroy the partisans. For rapid identification of "friend and foe," all personnel taking part in "Operation Hornung" were to wear a white band on the left sleeve, or a red band if wearing camouflage clothing. After the conclusion of the operation on 26 February 1943 it was reported that 1,272 partisans had been killed, 1,211 suspected partisans shot and 104 prisoners taken. Once again, as in other German operations against partisans, the numbers are suggestive of executions.

The Radionov Battalion subsequently moved to Glubokoye, where it was to join the Blazhevich Battalion, formed in STALAG 319A on 11 December 1942, to form the SS Unit Drushina. Formed under the command of former NKVD Major Blazhevich, the battalion had previously been in training in the Gaydov area. The German commander of the SS Unit Drushina was *SS-Sturmbannführer* Reußner, a member of the SD. On 13 June 1943 *SS-Gruppenführer und Generalleutnant der Polizei* von Gottberg reported to the Reich Central Security Office that Reußner had succeeded in:

"very quickly welding this formation, consisting of 1,200 Russians, into a capable unit which can be relied upon in the battle against partisans."

In April 1943 the intelligence chief on the staff of the Senior SS and Police Commander "Central Russia and White Ruthenia" gave the SS Unit Drushina the code name "Tiger."

After transfer to Luzhki in May 1943, from 3 to 23 June the SS Unit Drushina took part in "Operation Cottbus" as part of Operations Group West under the Senior SS and Police Commander "Central Russia and White Ruthenia" *SS-Obergruppenführer und General der Waffen-SS* von dem Bach. On the German side a total of 16,662 men took part in this large-scale operation to clear the Polotsk – Borisov – Lepel area. The operation unleashed unbelievable brutality and led to unimaginable happenings. The frequent mining of the rear communications roads had led to the inhabitants becoming regarded as sympathetic to the partisans. Most of those suspected of being sympathizers were driven onto the mined roads, and it is estimated that 2,000 to 3,000 civilians were killed. A propaganda leader who was present described infernal scenes in which swine were running through empty villages carrying pieces of bodies. In approximately three weeks there were approximately 13,000 enemy dead and only 950 captured rifles. Once again, it appears to have been a case of executions of the inhabitants of the villages. On 18 June 1943 the Reich Commissar for the Eastern Land wrote to the Reich Minister for Occupied eastern Areas about "Operation Cottbus":

"That Jews received special handling requires no further discussion. That other things happened, as described in the General Commissar's report [Kube, author's note] of 1 June

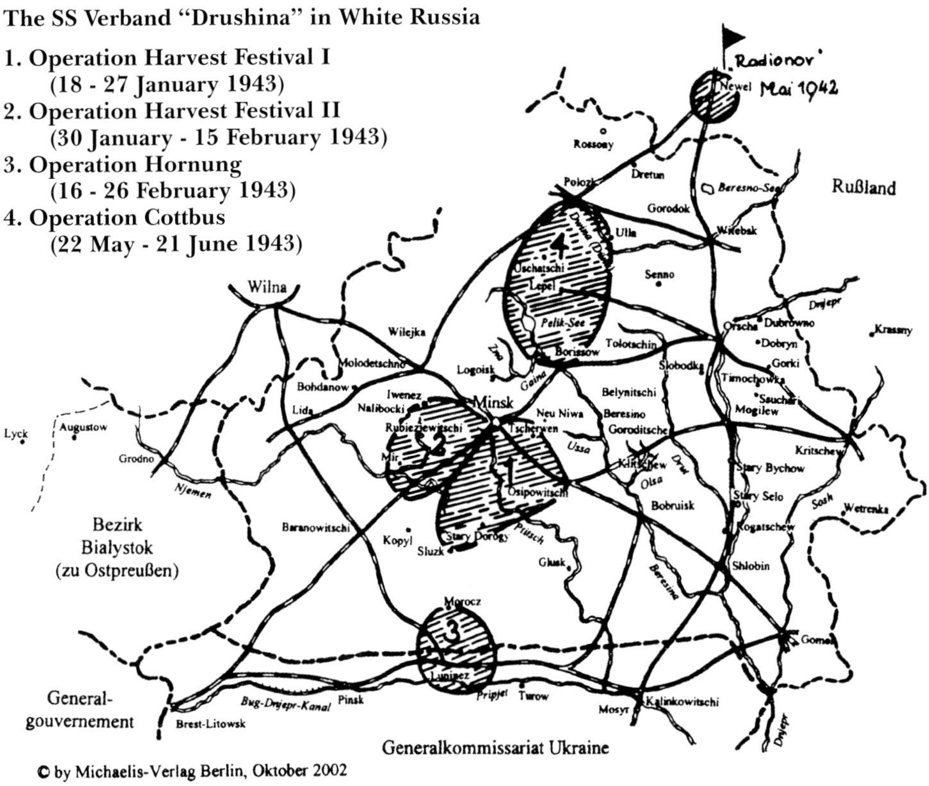

1943, seems scarcely believable, however. What is Katyn in comparison? One can only imagine that such occurrences are known on the other side and that they are made the most of there! Such propaganda will probably be ineffective simply because the listeners and readers will not be ready to believe it.

The struggle against the bandits is also taking on highly questionable forms, if the pacification and exploitation of the various areas is the objective of our policy. In my opinion, with few exceptions the suspected bandits killed in "Operation Cottbus", 5,000 according to the report of 5 June, would have been suitable for forced labor in the Reich.

I am not unaware of the difficulties resulting from communications problems which make it very difficult to tell friend from foe in such clearing operations. It should be possible, however, to avoid atrocities and bury those liquidated. Locking men, women and children up in barns and setting them on fire seems to me to be an unsuitable method of combating partisans unless one is trying to wipe out the population. This method is unworthy of the German cause and severely damages our image. I request that you take the necessary steps from there."

Even though *SS-Gruppenführer und Generalleutnant der Polizei* von Gottberg wrote about the reliability of SS Unit Drushina while "Operation Cottbus" was still going on, what the Russian volunteers saw during this operation had an enormous impact. They had volunteered to fight against the inhuman Stalinist system and now had to witness the brutality of the Germans. Soon afterwards, when desertion became possible, on 13 August 1943 approximately 400 members of the SS unit under the command of Radionov deserted to the partisans and subsequently fought against the German occupation forces as the 1st Anti-Fascist Brigade.[68] In his memoirs *SS-Brigadeführer* Schellenberg, the former head of Department VI of the Reich Central Security Office, recalled of Radionov:

"I spoke with Gill [pseudonym for Radionov, author's note] a number of times and could not ward off the suspicion that his anti-Soviet position had faltered. The manner in which he criticized the German leadership's mistakes in Russia in general—with special reference to German propaganda about Russian sub-humanity—and against the population and prisoners of war in particular, had a certain undertone which had to arouse suspicion."

SS Unit Drushina was disbanded immediately after these desertions. The remaining approximately 500 men formed the 1st Guards Battalion of the Russian Liberation Army (ROA) in the Pskov area. Its commander was Colonel Ivanov, deputy commander Colonel Sakharov, and chief-of-staff Colonel Kromiadi.

Epilogue

Himmler's desire to enlarge the *Waffen-SS* with Russian units in the summer of 1944 was a failure. If the former volunteers had by then lost any interest in standing on the German side, their motivation for fighting in the ranks of the *Waffen-SS* or police was even less! The main reason was Hitler's eastern policy. Since 1941 the Russian volunteers had had plenty of opportunities to see Germany's position relative to Eastern Europe. The treatment of Soviet prisoners of war, eastern workers, and civilians not only led to demotivation and resignation, but to hate and loathing as well. Two Russian officers are offered as representative: after visiting Germany, Major Turlakov declared to Kaminski that he believed he was on the wrong side and committed suicide, and the commander of the Radionov Battalion deserted to the partisans with his men after witnessing the German massacre of the White Russian population during "Operation Cottbus."

If there had been a National-Socialist movement in Russia, the men would have been fighting bolshevism and Stalin for a sovereign national state. As Hitler could not accept this, the volunteers were opportunists or—even if against their will—simple mercenaries. And a study by the Army General Staff found in 1942 that:

"*The Russian has always [...] been a poor mercenary.*"

Appendices

Appendix 1

The Russian Mentality

In autumn 1941 *Oberstleutnant* Gehlen,[69] a group leader in the Army General Staff department "Foreign Armies East," commissioned a study of the Russian people. The study was first presented to officers of the German general staff in Vinnitsa. It gave revealing impressions and demonstrated the differences between the Russian and German mentality which still exist today:

"[...] In the mental image of the Russian one first encounters a striking width of the emotional field, meaning a great wealth of feelings and effects, of motivations, which play a decisive role in the behavior of the Russian. The characteristic features are powerful feelings and motivations rising to extreme intensity, a frequent and sudden shift between emotional states with a great variation in their quality and content.

With the Russians, therefore, we experience brutality as well as the most tender sympathy, deep faith together with the crassest materialism, vivid enthusiasm next to apathy, bravery and cowardice, universal will and sudden failure. Today we are all witnesses to these conflicting natures in the breast of the Russian people! These opposite natures are both a strength and a weakness, and the Russian is conscious of both. Yet he does not perceive the strength within himself to balance out these contradictions; perhaps he doesn't even want to. [...]

The western man, by "making an effort", tries to overcome suffering through action, while the Russian has learned to endure it. The distant, dark powers of violence, the hopeless struggle against epidemics and the forces of nature, perhaps even his religion have taught him that suffering is an unavoidable part of his life. [...]

The Russian farmer:

The Russian farmer and the Russian village are both familiar phenomena. We know that the farmer has become much poorer since Russia became a so-called farmer's republic. We know that the farmer owns practically nothing apart from a garden plot, a cow and a few hens. And it is known that the farmer hates the collective system, because it has turned farmers into rural proletarians. The general flight from the land is characteristic of the "internal Soviet success in the field of agrarian politics". The Russian farmer is politically disinterested. He has just one desire—a piece of land of his own. It matters little to him who governs. He will welcome any authority which gives him land and is more just than its predecessor. The rural proletarian will again become the farmer and lead his own life, and therefore all theories about a "Russian mass soul" are wrong and irrelevant. [...]

The worker:

If one compares today's worker with that of the First World War, one must plainly admit that today he seems much more enlightened and has learned much as a specialized worker. Nevertheless, in terms of performance he cannot compare to the German worker in the long run. Neither the joy he takes in his work nor his income measure up to European standards. [...]

Space and Numbers:

As scales are the topic of discussion, it seems fitting to quickly touch on the question of space and numbers, which have strongly influenced the character of the Russian man.

The Russian man is the product of the endless spaces into which he is born. Coming from a small space, the European must adapt himself, both intellectually and emotionally if he is to master his task in the east. […] The vastness of the Russian spaces, with their impenetrable forests and unconnected rivers, must have the effect of hampering any real progress and every equally strong will. […] In Russia the master is the one who commands space and masses. Perhaps we will now come to understand why to the Russians the fate of the individual has always been of secondary importance. […]

Perhaps it is appropriate at this point to thoroughly investigate the reasons for the bitter and determined resistance offered us by the Red commissars and soldiers. I have already answered these questions, in part in the German officer's gazette and also within the scope of this study.

The Russian has always been a poor mercenary but a good soldier; obedient to every authority, resigned to his fate and so undemanding—so frightfully undemanding!"

Appendix 2

The Russian National-Socialist Workers Party

On 25 November 1941 Constantine Voskoboynik, the mayor of Lokot, founded the Russian National-Socialist Party. After Voskoboynik's death Kaminski assumed control of the party, which had the following founding manifest:

"Citizens of Russia!

Our homeland—Russia—created by the tremendous efforts of our ancestors, is on the verge of collapse.

Millions of Russian sons have been destroyed in the current war. Millions of orphans, widows and grieving mothers are the result of this insane struggle.

Beautiful cities, villages, monuments to culture and art, created over centuries by the work and sweat of the Russian people have been turned into ashes. Never in its entire history has our people endured such torment and suffering.

The people of Russian know that the only guilty ones are the Bolsheviks under their bloodthirsty Stalin.

They lied to our people in 1917: they used the revolution begun by the people to seize power. They promised the farmers land, the workers the plants and factories, the entire people freedom of speech and the press. The people of Russia have had to pay for their gullibility with unprecedented suffering and sacrifice. Instead of land the farmers have received the slavery of the collective farm, the workers forced labor in plants and factories. Instead of freedom the people have been given a close-meshed net of prisons and concentration camps.

The Bolsheviks have sacrificed the 170 million Russian people to their mad international plans which are directed against all of humanity.

The people of Russia have never ceased their struggle against their bitterest foe, bolshevism—but without success. A tremendously large number of NKVD executioners, mainly Jews, have stifled every attempt at resistance.

Only now, with bolshevism weakened by the war and weapons in the hands of the people, is a realization of the efforts of the Russian people possible.

History will never again offer us such a favorable opportunity and if we do not take advantage of it, Russia will go under and our children and children's children will damn us. They will say, "For thousands of years there has been no more unfit generation than that which permitted the ruin of Russia."

Every citizen of Russia must understand and feel that he, too, is personally responsible for the fate of his homeland.

The saving of Russia is only possible if all of Russia's upright sons unite, willing to wage a sacrifice-filled struggle in a powerful organization (party), which would be capable of taking on the communist party. In the knowledge that only an organized power is capable of bringing down bloody bolshevism and rescuing the homeland from ruin, we join together in the National-Socialist Russian Workers Party under the command of B.W. Kaminski, an experienced fighter for the good of Russia, leader of the new party.

The NSRAP has set as its goals:

1. The destruction of the bloody Stalinist regime in Russia

2. The founding of a sovereign state, uniting all the peoples of Russia

3. Acknowledgement of the right of self-determination of the various Russian nationalities ready to establish independent states

4. Liquidation of the class differences artificially created by bolshevism through a just, social, working order to be created in the new Russia. Private property and private initiative will form the basis of economic policy.

5. The land must be turned over to the farmers for their own use.

6. The worker is to be turned from a proletarian in bondage into a free worker, who will also share in the profits.

7. The creative power of intelligence must be freed from political chains. Full freedom of speech and the press.

8. All property rights of former estate owners and capitalists (Russian as well as foreign) are null and void.

Against the Jewish internationalist ideas we offer the national idea, the love of country and people. We bind ourselves by a solemn oath to give all our strength and also our lives for the attainment of these goals, for the salvation of our land.

We call upon all upright sons of Russia, to whom the homeland is dear and who wish to see its people free and happy, to support the new Russian leadership and to fortify the strength of the National Russian Liberation Army—the true representative of the new regime.

Organizational committee of the NSRAP:

Mossin, Bakshansky, Vasyukov, Voshshile, Khomutov."

The German leadership always strictly opposed political agitation in the eastern territories, but as Kaminski pursued no separatist agenda, instead professing a close alignment of his National-Socialist movement with the German Reich, Hitler tolerated the NSRAP. In doing so he probably had in mind the old Roman proverb "*divide et impera*" (divide and conquer). This sentiment was also expressed by the Army High Command—which characterized it as "*free play of forces*"—in a report on the NSRAP on 3 July 1944. It should be noted, however, that the OKH itself made several incorrect interpretations. It declared that the party was only represented in White Russia, and if it was written that the totally desolate and discouraged Kaminski movement was the "*most powerful of the anti-Bolshevik organizations*" that is more than characteristic of the situation at that time:

"*The NSRAP has grown further. At the present time it is the most powerful of the anti-Bolshevik organizations on the central and northern part of the eastern theater of war.*

So far the principle of free play of forces has been applied to the various anti-Bolshevik movements in the eastern area. Consideration should also be given to this principle in the future, but this should not lead to an attitude toward the NSRAP, an organization which has proved itself in the struggle against bolshevism, which results in it failing to receive the necessary support. Minor considerations are not appropriate when what is at stake is the gaining and motivation of valuable forces which can take pressure off the German armed services in their difficult struggle against bolshevism..."

From 1942 Kaminski emphasized the military sector with the formation and employment of the "RONA" People's Brigade, and the importance of the NSRAP went into a steady decline until, by the summer of 1944, it was essentially powerless. On 24 July 1944 the Army General Staff wrote to the Department of Foreign Armies East:

"As a result of the military events of the past weeks the matter has lost importance to the army groups..."

The Reich Minister for the Occupied Eastern Areas appeared to be equally disinterested when he declared on 26 July 1944:

"At present Kaminski's following is believed to be approximately 27,000 persons. The brigade itself consists of about 3,000-4,000 armed men and with their families 8,000-10,000 people. The rest are party members of Kaminski, who is known to have created a National-Socialist Russian Party. We have no particular political interest in this party..."

With the death of Kaminski in August 1944 the NSRAP also ceased to exist.

Appendix 3

Chronology

29. Waffen-Grenadier-Division der SS "RONA" (russische Nr. 1)

10/41	The mayor of Lokot, Voskoboynik, forms his own police service.
12/41	Unnoticed, the police service becomes the people's defense.
01/42	German railway pioneers come upon the Russian people's defense in the woods south of Briansk. After Voskoboynik's death, Kaminski assumes the office of mayor and leader of the people's defense.
03/42	Strength of the people's defense: approx. 1,400 men.
07/42	Kaminski becomes administrator of a self-governed district and RONA brigade commander.
09/42	Strength of the People's Defense Brigade: approx. 6,000 men.
12/42	Strength of the People's Defense Brigade: approx. 9,000 men.
01-02/43	Participation in "Operations Polar Bear I - III".
02/43	The VIII Battalion sees action near Dimitrovsk.
05/43	Participation in "Operations Gypsy Baron" and "Freischütz."
06/43	Participation in "Operation Freischütz."
08/43	Evacuation of the population of the self-governed district and of the RONA to Lepel (White Russia).
10/43	Participation in "Operation Hubertus"
04-05/44	Participation in "Operation Spring Festival" Evacuation of the civilian population and RONA to Dyatlovo.
06/44	Order to establish the *Waffen-Sturmbrigade der SS "RONA"*
07/44	One battle group sees action as part of Battle Group von Gottberg. Evacuation of the civilian population and RONA in the direction of Slovakia.
08/44	Participation in suppression of the Warsaw uprising. Order for the formation of the *29. Waffen-Grenadier-Division der SS "RONA" (russische Nr. 1)*.

11/44	Separation of the civilian population from the soldiers and their transfer to Münsingen to the 600. Infantry Division (russische)

30. Waffen-Grenadier-Division der SS (russische Nr. 2)

06/44	Formation of the Police Brigade "Siegling" in East Prussia.
08/44	Order for the formation of the 30. Waffen-Grenadier-Division der SS. Transfer to France. Anti-terrorist operations.
09/44	Reorganization of the division in Defense District V / formation of two fortification construction regiments with about 2,400 unreliable division members.
11/44	Action in the Burgundian Gate.
12/44	Transfer to the Upper Pfalz for reorganization.
01/45	Disbandment of the 30. Waffen-Grenadier-Division der SS. Order for the formation of a Waffen-Grenadier-Brigade der SS (weissruthenische Nr. 1).
04/45	Disbandment of the division / formation of a Police Battalion Siegling.

SS Unit "Drushina"

03/42	Action "Zeppelin"
04/42	Formation of the Radionov Battalion.
05/42	Transfer to the Nevel area.
11/42	1st Company deserts to the partisans.
12/42	Formation of the Blazhevich Battalion.
01/43	Participation in "Harvest Festival I".
02/43	Participation in "Harvest Festival II". Participation in "Operation Hornung"
03/43	transfer into the Glubokoye area. Formation of the SS Unit "Drushina" by combining both battalions.
05/43	Transfer of the SS unit to Luzhki.
06/43	Participation in "Operation Cottbus."
08/43	Desertion of more than 400 men to the partisans.
09/43	Disbandment of the SS Unit "Drushina" and formation of the 1st Guards Battalion of RONA from the remnants of the SS Unit.

Appendix 4

Military Postal Numbers and Command Positions

29. Waffen-Grenadier-Division der SS "RONA" (russische Nr 1)

Commander	M. P. N.* 45 155	*Waffen-Brigadeführer und Generalmajor der Waffen-SS* Kaminski
		SS-Brigadeführer u. Gen.Maj. der Polizei
Diehm		
		SS-Gruppenführer und Gen.Lt. der W-SS Jürs
Liaison Officer		*SS-Sturmbannführer* Reussner
Chief of Staff		*Waffen-Obersturmbannführer* Shavykin
Ia		*Waffen-Sturmbannführer* Frolov
Ic		*Waffen-Hauptsturmführer* Kapkayev

30. Waffen-Grenadier-Division der SS (russische Nr. 2)

Commander	M. P. N. 14 471	*SS-Obersturmbannführer* Hans Siegling
Ia		*SS-Hauptsturmführer* Johannes Deutschbein
Ib		*SS-Sturmbannführer* Franz Henningfeld
IIa		*SS-Hauptsturmführer* Schneider
H.Q. Commander		*SS-Hauptsturmführer* Rall
III		*SS-Obersturmführer* Dr. Erwin Vrbka
IVa		*SS-Sturmbannführer* Bruno Pauli
IVb		*SS-Sturmbannführer* Dr. Erich Windisch
IVc		*SS-Obersturmführer* Dr. Heuer
V		*SS-Hauptsturmführer* Peter Arimont
VI		*SS-Obersturmbannführer* Noftiz

* M. P. N. - Military Postal Number

Waffen-Grenadier-Regiment der SS 75 (russische Nr. 4)

Commander	M. P. N. 08 385	*SS-Sturmbannführer* Hans Österreich
I Battalion	M. P. N. 66 415	
II Battalion	M. P. N. 66 408	
III Battalion	M. P. N. 67 827	

Waffen-Grenadier-Regiment der SS 76 (russische Nr. 5)

Commander	M. P. N. 01 069	*SS-Sturmbannführer* Gautz *SS-Sturmbannführer* Schmidt *SS-Hauptsturmführer* Ernst Sieloff
I Battalion	M. P. N. 64 868	
II Battalion	M. P. N. 67 283	
III Battalion	M. P. N. 65 794	

Waffen-Grenadier-Regiment der SS 77 (russische Nr. 6)

Commander	M. P. N. 03 844	*SS-Sturmbannführer* Mocha
I Battalion	M. P. N. 65 253	
II Battalion	M. P. N. 67 002	
III Battalion	M. P. N. 66 134	
SS Artillery Battalion 30	M. P. N. 05 607	*SS-Hauptsturmführer* Glaser *SS-Hauptsturmführer* Riehs
SS Reconnaissance Battalion 30	M. P. N. 31 251	*SS-Sturmbannführer* Hofmann *SS-Obersturmführer* Dr. Merkulow
SS Fusilier Company		*SS-Sturmbannführer* Hubert Marbach
SS Pioneer Company		*SS-Hauptsturmführer* Wolf
SS Signals Company		*SS-Hauptsturmführer* Müller
SS Medical Company		*SS-Hauptsturmführer* Dr. Werner Fosgreen
SS Armored Reconnaissance Company		*SS-Hauptsturmführer* Erwin Kirchner
SS Field Replacement Battalion 30	M. P. N. 41 526	*SS-Hauptsturmführer* Bindl

Waffen-Grenadier-Brigade der SS (weissruthenische Nr. 1)

Commander	M. P. N. 14 471	*SS-Standartenführer* Hans Siegling
Ia		*SS-Sturmbannführer* Hans Deutschbein
Battalion Commanders		*SS-Sturmbannführer* Albert Löffler
		SS-Sturmbannführer Ernst Niepel
		SS-Hauptsturmführer Reinhold Meusel

Appendix 5

Short Biographies

Ekkehard Altmann was born in Schönlanke on 15 April 1906 and joined the NSDAP on 1 May 1933 (No. 1,971,719). Serving as a police officer, in 1941 he achieved the rank of *Hauptmann der Schutzpolizei* and when his rank was aligned with those of the SS he became an *SS-Hauptsturmführer*. On 30 January 1945 Altmann was promoted to *SS-Sturmbannführer* retroactive to 21 December 1944 and assigned to the *30. Waffen-Grenadier-Division der SS (russische Nr. 2)*.

Fritz Arlt was born in Niedercunnersdorf on 12 April 1912 and in 1929 became a member of the *Jungvolk* of the Hitler Youth. After graduation, in 1932 he began studies at the University of Leipzig, and in 1936 he went to work in the District Office for Racial and Population Policy in Breslau. Two years later he began teaching at the University of Breslau. After the campaign in Poland, Dr. Arlt worked in the government of the Generalgouvernement. He joined the *Waffen-SS* in 1940 and became an officer in the staff of the *Reichsführer-SS*, serving as Reich Commissar for the Promotion of German Folklore. In 1943 Dr. Arlt reported to the *SS-Panzer-Grenadier-Division "Das Reich,"* and while serving with that unit was wounded near Yampol in 1944. He was transferred to the SS Head Office and took over the Volunteer Control Center "East" (Balts, Ukrainians, White Ruthenians, and Cossacks). In the last weeks of the war Dr. Arlt was assigned to the *14. Waffen-Grenadier-Division der SS (ukrainische Nr. 1)* as liaison officer.

Erich von dem Bach (-Zelewski) was born in Lauenburg on 1 March 1889. He fought in the First World War and was decorated with the Iron Crosses, First and Second Class. In 1919 he served in the Eastern Border Guard and Upper Silesia. He left the service in 1924 as a *Leutnant*. In 1930 he joined the NSDAP, and one year later the SS (No. 9,831). On 15 December 1934 Bach attained the rank of an *SS-Gruppenführer* and became SS Senior Sector Commander "Northeast" (East Prussia). After conflicts with *Gauleiter* Koch he was relieved, and on 15 February 1936 took over Senior Sector "Southeast" (Silesia). On 28 June 1938 he was named Senior SS and Police Commander "Southeast." On 10 April 1941 he received the supplementary rank of *Generalleutnant der Polizei*. Three weeks later Bach was transferred to the personal staff of the *Reichsführer-SS*, and on 22 June 1941 became Senior SS and Police Commander "Central Russia." Effective 9 November 1941 he was promoted to the rank of *SS-Obergruppenführer und General der Polizei*. Having been named Commissioner of the *Reichsführer-SS* for Anti-Bandit Operations on 23 October 1942, on 21 June 1943 he was placed in command of all anti-bandit units. From 1 July 1944 he was permitted to bear the title of *General der Waffen-SS*. After the retreat from White Russia, from August to mid-October 1944 he led Corps Group von dem Bach, which was responsible for suppressing the Warsaw uprising. On 30 September 1944 he was awarded the Knight's Cross of the Iron Cross for his actions. From 10 November 1944 until 25 January 1945 Bach commanded the corps headquarters of XIV SS Army Corps, which was deployed on the Upper Rhine. From 26 January to 10 February 1945 the command of X SS Army Corps assembled in Posen-West Prussia. One week later he took over the so-called "Oder Corps." Bach was held prisoner by the Allies until 1950, and at the Nuremberg Trials he testified against the principal war criminals as a witness for the prosecution. Not until 1961 was he sentenced to 4½ years in prison for manslaughter. One year later he was given life imprisonment for multiple murders. He died in prison on 8 March 1972.

Gottlob Berger was born in Gerstetten on 16 July 1896 and joined the NSDAP in 1922. From 1932 he led the SA Sub-Group Wurttemberg, and on 30 January 1936 was taken into the SS as an *Oberführer*. On 20 April 1939 Berger attained the rank of an *SS-Brigadeführer* and was made head of the SS Replacement Office. Two years later he was promoted to *SS-Gruppenführer* and assigned to the chief of the SS Head Office. On 21 June 1943 Berger became an *SS-Obergruppenführer* and *General der Waffen-SS*. He held numerous positions during the war, including that of Prisoner of War Affairs.

Friedrich-Gustav Bernhard was born in Bad Harzburg on 5 October 1888, and on 15 March 1909 joined the military as an officer candidate. On 22 August 1910 he was promoted to *Leutnant* and assigned to the 2nd Railway Regiment. He served in the *Reichsheer* in the First World War. On 15 October 1935 *Oberstleutnant* Bernhard became commander of II Corps signal units. Promoted to *Oberst* on 1 August 1936, he took part in the Second World War, first as army signals officer in Headquarters, 7th Army, and from 1 November 1939 as army signals officer in Headquarters, 18th Army. On 1 August 1940 Bernhard was promoted to signals officer of Army Group A and promoted to *Generalmajor*. In autumn 1941 he was named commander of 2nd Panzer Army's rear army area, and in April 1942 Korück 532. Promoted to *Generalleutnant* on 1 August 1942 and awarded the German Cross in Gold on 17 March 1944, Bernhard was hanged in Russia in 1945.

Karl Bornemann was born in Austria on 15 September 1885, and on 1 October 1906 joined Infantry Regiment 99 of the Imperial Army as a volunteer. On 1 January 1908 he was promoted to *Leutnant der Reserve*, and on 1 November 1910 he became an active officer. After taking part in the First World War Bornemann served in the Federal Austrian Army, and following promotion to *Generalmajor* on 26 June 1937 he commanded the 2nd Austrian Division. At the outset of the Second World War he commanded Division No. 148, and from 10 January 1940 Special Purpose Division Command 442. While in this position he was promoted to *Generalleutnant*. From 5 January to 31 March 1944 he commanded Special Purpose Division Command 410. Decorated with the German Cross in Gold, Bornemann subsequently became *Wehrmacht* commander of Würzburg, and on 15 March 1945 entered the officer reserve in Defense District XVII.

Sergei Bunyatshenko was born in the Ukraine and became an active soldier. At the start of the Second World War he commanded the Soviet 398th Rifle Division. On 5 September 1942 he was sentenced to death by Stalin for prematurely destroying a railway line and hampering the use of an armored train. After he was pardoned, Bunyatshenko deserted to the Germans and served in Special Eastern Headquarters 721. In 1943 he took over a Russian unit in France and fought successfully on the invasion front. In autumn 1944 he was named commander of the 600th Infantry Division (Russian) with the rank of *Generalmajor*. Captured on 10 May 1945, Bunyatshenko was hanged in Moscow on 1 August 1946.

Johannes Deutschbein was born in Euskirchen on 9 September 1913, and after completing school in 1932 began a career as a salesman. He joined the NSDAP on 1 May 1933 (No. 3,504,349), and on 1 October the SA (No. 162,951). He moved over to active police service, and in 1939 achieved the rank of *Leutnant der Schutzpolizei* in Berlin Police Battalion 5 and simultaneously *SS-Sturmmann* in the General SS in the *58. Standarte*. On 1 September 1939 Deutschbein was named *Oberleutnant der Schutzpolizei*. From 17 September 1941 to 30 April 1943 he worked in the staff of the Senior SS and Police Commander "Caucasus" as supply officer (Ib). At that time his SS rank was harmonized with his rank in the Schutzpolizei. Promoted again, his rank was: *SS-Hauptsturmführer und HPR der Schutzpolizei*. From 1 May to 5 July 1943 he was adjutant to the Senior SS and Police Commander "Central Russia and White Ruthenia." On 30 July 1943 Deutschbein was wounded in an anti-partisan operation while serving as a staff officer (6 July to 5 November 1943). From 6 November 1943 until the summer of 1944 he was 1st General Staff Officer with the Senior SS and Police Commander "Central Russia and White Ruthenia." Effective 1 August 1944 Deutschbein assumed the same position with the 30. Waffen-Grenadier-Division der SS (russische Nr. 2). Deutschbein was decorated with the 1 October 1938 Commemorative Medal, the East Medal, the Wound Badge in Black, and the War Merit Crosses 1st and 2nd Class with Swords as well as the Merit Decoration for Members of the Eastern Peoples 2nd Class in Silver (14 January 1945).

Christoph Diehm was born on 1 March 1892 and participated in the First World War as an officer in the 60th Prussian Infantry Division. After serving in a *Freikorps* after the war he joined the SA, and on 1929 became adjutant to the SA commander in Wurttemberg. On 22 March 1932 Diehm was taken into the SS with the rank of Oberführer. After just two years he was an *SS-Brigadeführer* and commanded SS Sector XIX, and until 1939 SS Sector I. Diehm was attached to the staff of the SS Senior Sector West. He was then attached to the Reich Central Security Office until 1943. From June 1943 until 25 July 1944 he held the post of SS and Police Commander Lvov. As of 20 August 1944 Diehm was initially considered for command of the *29. Waffen-Grenadier-Division der SS "RONA" (russische Nr. 1)*; instead, however, he went to the SS Head Office, and on 9 November 1944 was given the supplementary rank of *Generalmajor der Waffen-SS*.

Erich Ehrlinger was born in Giengen in 1910, and after school studied law. He took his first state exams in 1933 and, after joining the NSDAP on 15 April 1931, worked in the SA Office of Higher Education. From 1 July 1934 he led the SA Sports School, and on 22 June 1936 was accepted into the SS. First employed in the Würzburg SD sector, by September 1935 Ehrlinger was working in the SD Head Office in Berlin. In 1938 followed transfer to Vienna and Prague, and in 1939 participation in the Polish Campaign in an *Einsatzkommando* (operational detachment). Afterwards he became a department head with the Commander of the Security Police and SD in Warsaw. In March 1941 Ehrlinger was transferred to the Reich Central Security Office (RSHA), and from June 1941 he commanded Special Detachment Ib of *Einsatzgruppe A*. On 9 December of the same year he took over the office of commander of the Security Police and SD in Kiev. Nine months later Ehrlinger became "Commissioner of the Head of the Security Police and SD with the Commanding General of Security Forces and Commander of Army Group Center" and simultaneously head of *Einsatzgruppe B*. On 1 April 1944 he was transferred back to the RHSA as head of Department I. On 9 November 1944 he was promoted to SS-Oberführer. In December 1961 Ehrlinger was sentenced to 12 years imprisonment for participating in Nazi war crimes. He was released from prison in 1965 during the appeal proceedings, which were abandoned in 1969.

Reinhard Gehlen was born in Erfurt on 3 April 1902 and entered military service on 20 April 1920. He was commissioned as a *Leutnant* with the 3rd Artillery Regiment on 1 December 1923. From 10 November 1938 he was commander of 8th Company, Artillery Regiment 18, and from 1 September 1939 1st General Staff Officer of the 213th Infantry Division. At the end of October 1939 Gehlen was transferred to the Army General Staff, and in autumn 1940 became a group leader in the Army General Staff's operations section. Following promotion to *Oberstleutnant* on 1 July 1941, from spring 1942 Gehlen worked as head of the Foreign Armies East Department. There, on 1 July 1942, he was promoted to *Oberst*. After receiving the German Cross in Silver, on 1 December 1944 he was promoted to *Generalmajor*.

Werner Freiherr von und zu Gilsa was born in Berlin on 4 March 1889. In 1909 he was a *Leutnant* in the Guards Fusilier Regiment. After the First World War he served in the *Reichswehr*, and on 1 October 1936 became commander of the 9th Infantry Regiment with the rank of *Oberstleutnant*. On 1 March 1937 von und zu Gilsa was promoted to *Oberst*. Promoted to *Generalmajor* (1 February 1941), he commanded the 216th Infantry Division until 4 April 1943. Further promotions followed, to *Generalleutnant* on 1 October 1942 and *General der Infanterie* on 1 July 1943. While holding the latter rank he commanded LXXXIX Army Corps. Following this, he was the military commander of Dresden and commanding general of the Gilsa Corps. Decorated with the Knight's Cross with Oak Leaves, he committed suicide in 1945.

Fritz Glaser was born in Schumberg/Desse (Sudetenland) on 19 March 1913. After completing elementary and high school he studied for ten semesters at the Academy for Music. He served in the 13th Artillery Regiment of the Czech Army from 1 October 1936 to 11 October 1938. One week later he entered the 28. SS-Standarte (No. 306,865), and in November of the same year joined the NSDAP (No. 6,432,246). On 7 December 1938 he began serving with the Hamburg Police. Effective 1 June 1941 Glaser became an active SS officer with the rank of *SS-Untersturmführer*. On 1 April 1942 he was promoted to *SS-Obersturmführer* and placed in command of the *4. SS-Polizei-Panzer-Grenadier-Division*. On 20 April 1944 he was promoted to *SS-Hauptsturmführer*, and two months later was transferred to the SS Artillery Training and Replacement Regiment. On 20 August 1944 Glaser was assigned to the *30. Waffen-Grenadier-Division der SS (russische Nr. 2)*, and on 20 November was placed in command of the infantry battalion.

Kurt von Gottberg was born in Preußisch Wilten on 11 February 1896. After graduation he joined the army and took part in the First World War from 1914, winning the Iron Crosses, First and Second Class. Discharged as an *Oberleutnant*, from 1919 to 1924 he was a member of the Erhard Brigade. He joined the NSDAP and the SS (No. 45,913) in 1932, and from 1937 to 1939 worked in the Race and Settlement Head Office. As an *SS-Oberführer* he led the land office in Prague. From 1 October 1940 until 21 July 1942 Gottberg was head of the requisitioning office in the SS Head Office. With promotion to *SS-Brigadeführer* and *Generalmajor der Polizei* he took over the post of SS and Police Commander "White Ruthenia," and on 24 March 1943 he became deputy to the Senior SS and Police Commander "Central Russia." On 15 July 1943 he was promoted to *SS-Gruppenführer* and *Generalleutnant der Polizei*. Nine days after assuming the position of Senior SS and Police Commander "Central Russia" on 21 June 1944 followed promotion to *SS-Obergruppenführer* and *General der Waffen-SS und Polizei*. On 20 July 1944 von Gottberg was awarded the Knight's Cross. Captured by the Allies, on 31 May 1945 he committed suicide in Flensburg.

Heinrich Jürs was born on 17 January 1897 and was an early member of the SS (membership number 11, 362). On 30 January 1933 he received the rank of *SS-Untersturmführer*, and on 3 September was promoted to *SS-Obersturmführer*. Soon afterwards, on 24 December, Jürs was promoted to *SS-Hauptsturmführer*. Further promotions followed unusually quickly: *SS-Sturmbannführer* on 12 April 1934; *SS-Obersturmbannführer* on 17 June 1934; *SS-Standartenführer* on 20 March 1935; and *SS-Oberführer* on 30 January 1936. From 1937 he was commander of SS Sector XXXII, and on 30 January 1939 was promoted *SS-Brigadeführer*. On 1 October 1940 Jürs received the rank of a *SS-Standartenführer der Reserve der Waffen-SS*, and until 1943 served as head of Department II in the SS Head Office. On 21 June 1943 he was promoted to *SS-Gruppenführer* and *Generalleutnant der Polizei*. Without receiving any additional promotions in the *Waffen-SS*, on 18 January 1945 the *SS-Standartenführer der Reserve der Waffen-SS* was promised promotion to the rank of *Generalleutnant der Waffen-SS*.

Bronislav Kaminski was born in Vitebsk on 16 June 1899, the son of a Pole and a German. He studied engineering in Leningrad and subsequently worked in the paint industry. Already an opponent of Stalin in the 1920s, in 1929 he signed the so-called Bukharin Declaration opposing Soviet agricultural policy. In August 1935 he was arrested for alleged contact with Polish and German agents and was banned to the Urals for ten years. From the Butirka Prison in Moscow he was taken to the Soviet concentration camp in Nishi-Tagirski/Chelyabinsk in the Urals. His mother's banishment ended in 1941. Kaminski was forced to settle in Lokot and worked as an engineer in the local distillery. There he met Constantine Voskoboynik, who opposed the Soviet regime and wanted to establish a national-socialist Russian state. After Voskoboynik's death on 8 January 1942, Kaminski took over the job of mayor and leadership of the Russian National-Socialist Party. During 1942 Kaminski became the leader of a self-governed district, and on 19 July 1942 was promoted to brigade commander of the local people's defense by the commander-in-chief of the 2nd Panzer Army, *Generaloberst* Schmidt. From November 1942 he was awarded several decorations for bravery for members of the eastern peoples, and on 27 January 1944 he was awarded the Iron Crosses, First and Second Class by *General* Burgdorf of the OKH. With events moving rapidly, Himmler decided to incorporate Russian units into the *Waffen-SS* and on 1 August 1944 he named Kaminski *Waffen-Brigadeführer* and *Generalmajor der Waffen-SS* and placed him in command of the *29. Waffen-Grenadier-Division der SS "RONA" (russische Nr. 1)*, which was then being formed. *SS-Obergruppenführer* and *General der Waffen-SS und Polizei* von dem Bach, who was present, also awarded Kaminski the Partisan Warfare Badge. Kaminski spoke out against the use of his soldiers against the Polish *Armija Krajowa* and their deployment in the west, and the German command considered him an uncomfortable troublemaker. When Russian soldiers in Warsaw stepped out of line against German civilians, Himmler ordered that "*the Kaminski problem be solved.*" On 28 August 1944 Kaminski was shot in Litzmannstadt by order of *SS-Obergruppenführer* and *General der Waffen-SS* von dem Bach. To cover up the act, a rumor was spread that Kaminski had been shot by Polish partisans.

Günther von Kluge was born in Posen on 30 October 1882 and subsequently joined the military as a cadet. A *Leutnant* in Field Artillery Regiment 46 on 23 March 1901, he participated in the First World War as a staff officer and in the *Reichswehr* commanded Artillery Regiment 2 as an *Oberst* (1 February 1920). Promoted to *Generalmajor* on 1 February 1933, on 1 October Kluge became Inspector of Signals Troops. Promotion to *Generalleutnant* followed on 1 April 1934, and six months later he took over the 6th Division. With this rank, on 1 April 1935 Kluge became commanding general of the VI Army Corps. Promotion to *General der Artillerie* followed on 1 August 1936. On 1 December 1938 he became commander-in-chief of *Gruppenkommando 6*. At the start of the Second World War the general commanded the 4th Army, and on 1 October 1939 he was promoted to the rank of *Generaloberst*. Following promotion to *Generalfeldmarschall* on 19 July 1940, Kluge was placed in command of Army Group Center on 19 December 1941. Decorated with the Knight's Cross with Oak Leaves and Swords, on 2 July 1944 the *Generalfeldmarschall* became Commander-in-Chief West, with Army Groups B and D under his command. On 16 August 1944, following the unsuccessful attempt on Hitler's life, he committed suicide in France.

Joachim Lemelsen was born in Berlin on 26 September 1888, and on 1 July 1907 he began his military service as an officer candidate. On 19 November 1908 he received his *Leutnant*'s patent with Field Artillery Regiment 40. After the First World War he served in the *Reichswehr*, and from 1 October 1934 he commanded the Artillery Instruction Regiment with the rank of *Oberst* (1 April 1934). On 1 April 1935 he took over the Officer School in Dresden, and on 1 March 1938 became commander of the 29th Division with the rank of *Generalmajor* (1 April 1937). Promoted to *Generalleutnant* on 1 April 1939, from 29 May 1940 he commanded the 5th Panzer Division, and on 25 November assumed command of XXXXVII Panzer Corps. On 1 August 1940 he was promoted to *General der Artillerie* (retitled *General der Panzertruppen* on 4 June 1941). From 1 November to 31 December 1943 Lemelsen was deputy commander-in-chief of the 10th Army, and from 1 May 1944 commander-in-chief of the 1st Army. Decorated with the Knight's Cross with Oak Leaves, from 5 June to 24 October 1944 the *General* commanded the 14th Army. Lemelsen died in Göttingen in 1954.

Fritz Löffler was born in Leipzig on 29 March 1911, and after graduating from high school he joined the *Landespolizei* on 1 April 1931. He joined the NSDAP (No. 1,439,270) on 1 January 1933, and in 1935 attended a course for police officer candidates. On 20 April 1937 he was named *Leutnant der Schutzpolizei*. On 4 May 1937 Löffler was transferred Schneidemühl, and there on 30 January 1938 he was promoted to *Oberleutnant der Schutzpolizei*. On 1 July 1939 he joined the *Allgemeine-SS* with the rank of *SS-Obersturmführer* (SS No. 337,330), and on 10 September was promoted to *SS-Hauptsturmführer*. From 1 November 1939 he was assigned to the 1st Company, 22nd Police Battalion in Thorn "*to carry out special police tasks [...] in the liberated [Polish] region*." After the attack on the Soviet Union Löffler served as an *SS-Hauptsturmführer* and *Hauptmann der Schutzpolizei* with the SS and Police base Commander Mogilev, and for a time commanded Front Police Battalion 51. When the German retreat from the Soviet Union resulted in the elimination of numerous PNN, in late summer 1944 Löffler was attached to the Order Police Head Office, and on 21 December was promoted to *SS-Sturmbannführer*. On 24 January 1945 he was assigned to the *Waffen-Grenadier-Brigade der SS (weissruthenische Nr. 1)* as a battalion commander. Löffler's decorations included the Iron Cross Second Class, War Merit Cross Second Class, the East Medal, and the Bravery Decoration for Members of the Eastern Peoples 2nd Class in Silver.

Hubert Marbach was born on 9 December 1904 and was a member of the Upper Silesian *Freikorps* (II Battalion, Upper Silesian Volunteer Regiment 2). He joined the NSDAP on 1 October 1940 (No. 9,864,476), and from 30 October 1943 to summer 1944 served as a policeman in the occupied eastern territories. There Marbach won the Iron Cross Second Class, War Merit Cross Second Class, Infantry Assault Badge in Silver, and the Wound Badge in Black. After passing through the Döberitz Infantry School (17 December 1944 to 30 January 1945), *SS-Hauptsturmführer* and *Hauptmann der Schutzpolizei* Marbach was promoted to *SS-Sturmbannführer* with an effective date of 21 December 1944. On 24 January 1945 he was transferred to the *Waffen-Grenadier-Brigade der SS (weissruthenische Nr. 1)*.

Ernst Niepel was born on 9 October 1902. After passing through the Döberitz Infantry School (17 December 1944 to 20 January 1945), on 30 January 1945 *SS-Hauptsturmführer* and *Hauptmann der Schutzpolizei* Niepel was promoted to *SS-Sturmbannführer* with an effective date of 21 December 1944. On 24 January he was transferred to the *Waffen-Grenadier-Brigade der SS (weissruthenische Nr. 1)* as a battalion commander. His decorations included the War Merit Crosses First and Second Class and the Merit Decoration for Members of the Eastern Peoples First and Second Class in Silver.

Friedrich Platz was born in Freiburg/Breisgau on 10 October 1897 and joined the NSDAP on 1 April 1933 (No. 1,679,839). Serving as a policeman, in 1942 he worked as a Major der Schutzpolizei in Munich. After passing through the Infantry School in Döberitz (17 December 1944 to 20 January 1945) on 30 January Platz was promoted to *SS-Sturmbannführer* with an effective date of 21 December 1944. On 24 January 1945 he was transferred to the *Waffen-Grenadier-Brigade der SS (weissruthenische Nr. 1)*.

Heinz-Friedrich Reinefarth was born in Gnesen on 23 December 1903. After completing school, in 1923 he joined the *Freikorps Oberland*. In 1932 he joined the NSDAP (No. 1,268,933) and the SS (No. 56,634). After studying law, he worked as a lawyer and notary from 1932 to 1939. Joining the army on 1 September 1939, he was subsequently awarded the Iron Cross First and Second Class. On 25 June 1940, while serving as a *Feldwebel* and platoon commander with the 337th Infantry Regiment, he was awarded the Knight's Cross. Reinefarth was later badly wounded and was discharged from the *Wehrmacht* as medically unfit. He then entered the *Waffen-SS* with the rank of an *SS-Brigadeführer* and *Generalmajor der Waffen-SS und Polizei*, and from June 1942 until the middle of 1943 served as Inspector-General of the Administration of the Protectorate of Bohemia and Moravia. After this he became head of the legal section in the Order Police Headquarters. From 29 February 1944 until January 1945 Reinefarth was Senior SS and Police Commander "Warthe," having been promoted to *SS-Gruppenführer* and *Generalleutnant der Waffen-SS und Polizei* on 1 July 1944. During the Warsaw uprising he commanded a battle group in the "von dem Bach" Corps Group. On 30 September 1944 he became the 608th soldier to be awarded the Knight's Cross with Oak Leaves. From 1 February 1945 Reinefarth commanded Fortress Küstrin. After the war he was the mayor of Westerland and died on 7 May 1979.

Gerhard Reußner was born in Kiel on 3 August 1909, and from 1915 to 1924 attended the Hindenburg Secondary School in Berlin-Lichterfeld. From 1924 to 1927 he trained as a salesman with a large Berlin textiles concern. A member of the SA since 4 August 1925, on 1 May 1928 he became a member of the NSDAP (membership number 88,831). Reußner worked as a salesman from 1 October 1928 until he was released in June 1934. From June 1938 he found employment with the Berlin-Center Employment Office. In the period from 1935 to 1937 Reußner took part in several multi-week exercises with the 9th Infantry Regiment and was promoted to *Gefreite* and officer candidate. On 1 April 1939 the former *SA-Hauptführer* joined the SD Sub-Sector Greater Berlin as an *SS-Hauptsturmführer* (SS No. 306,622). In 1943 he was named commander of the newly-formed SS Unit "Drushina," and on 21 May of that year was awarded the Iron Cross, 2nd Class and the Bravery Decoration for Members of the Eastern Peoples 2nd Class in Silver. On 13 June 1943 *SS-Gruppenführer* and *Generalleutnant der Polizei* von Gottberg asked the Reich Central Security Officer for early promotion for Reußner:

"SS-Hauptsturmführer is the German commander of the entire Drushina unit, at present consisting of 1,200 men. Because of his above-average perceptive faculties and his firm political views he has succeeded in quickly turning this unit of Russians into a capable unit which can be relied upon in the struggle against the bandits."

On 9 November Reußner was promoted to *SS-Sturmbannführer*. When the People's Defense Brigade "RONA" was taken into the *Waffen-SS* he was named liaison officer to the SS Head Office. On 1 August 1944 Reußner was promoted to *SS-Obersturmbannführer* and decorated with the Iron Cross, 1st Class.

Paul Salitter was born on 15 December 1898, and on 1 May 1937 he joined the NSDAP (No. 4,924,415). After passing through the Döberitz Infantry School (17 December 1944 to 20 January 1945), on 30 January *SS-Hauptsturmführer* and *Hauptmann der Schutzpolizei* Salitter was promoted to *SS-Sturmbannführer* with an effective date of 21 December 1944. On 24 January 1945 he was transferred to the *Waffen-Grenadier-Brigade der SS (Weissruthenische Nr. 1)*. He received the following decorations, some in the First World War: Iron Cross, 2nd Class, Wound Badge in Black, Frontline Fighter Honor Cross, Memelland Medal, Police Merit Decoration Ist Grade and Air Defense Honor Badge IInd Grade.

Rudolf Schmidt was born in Berlin on 12 May 1886, and on 25 September 1906 he began his military service as an officer candidate. On 27 January 1908 he became a *Leutnant* in the 83rd Infantry Regiment. After serving in the First World War he became a member of the *Reichswehr*, and on 1 October 1937 became commander of the 1st Panzer Division with the rank of *Generalmajor* (1 October 1936). Promoted to *Generalleutnant* on 1 June 1938, on 2 February 1940 he became commander of the XXXIX Panzer Corps, and on 15 November 1941 of the 2nd Army. Named commander-in-chief of the 2nd Panzer Army, on 1 January 1942 he was promoted to *Generaloberst*. Decorated with the Knight's Cross with Oak Leaves, Schmidt retired on 30 September 1943 and died in Krefeld in 1957.

Hans Siegling was born on 24 December 1912 and as an adult joined the police service. On 30 January 1940 he achieved the rank of *Oberleutnant der Schutzpolizei*, and on 1 November 1941 *Hauptmann der Schutzpolizei*. With that rank he led Police Battalion 57 in the area of the General Commissariat "White Ruthenia." Among others, in 1943 the battalion took part in "Operations Franz," "Hornung," "Lenz South," and "Lenz North." *SS-Brigadeführer* and *Generalmajor der Polizei* Walter Schimana acknowledged the unit's efforts in these actions:

"*My special acknowledgement goes to the Ukrainian Police Battalion 57 led by Hauptmann der Schutzpolizei Siegling. At times up to its breast in the swamps, it repulsed powerful breakout attempts by the enemy thus making a significant contribution to the success of the operation. Particularly laudable is the heroism of Hauptmann der Schutzpolizei Pohl, killed while leading his company. Pursuing fleeing bandits across the Gaina, he was the first of his company to reach the other side, where he met a hero's death.*"

On 11 April 1944, as *Hauptmann der Schutzpolizei* and commander of Police Battalion 57, Siegling was awarded the German Cross in Gold, and as *SS-Sturmbannführer* and *Major der Schutzpolizei* became SS and Police Commander "White Ruthenia and Pripyat." Effective 1 August 1944 Himmler promoted Siegling to *SS-Obersturmbannführer* and *Oberstleutnant der Schutzpolizei* and commander of a police brigade with a strength of about 9,000 men. On 18 August 1944 he was selected to command the *30. Waffen-Grenadier-Division der SS (russische Nr. 2)*, then being formed. After the unit was finally disbanded in April 1945, Siegling went on to command another police battalion which saw action as part of the 38th Grenadier Division "Nibelungen."

Helmuth Weidling was born in Halberstadt on 2 November 1891, and in 1911 joined the Imperial Army as an officer candidate. After serving in the First World War and the *Reichswehr*, from 10 November 1938 *Oberst* Weidling commanded the 56th Artillery Regiment. Subsequent commands included the 20th Artillery Regiment and Arko 128. Promoted to *Generalmajor*, on 1 January 1942 Weidling took over the 86th Infantry Division. Promoted to *Generalleutnant* on 1 January 1943 and *General der Artillerie* on 1 January 1944, from 20 October 1943 to 20 July 1944 he commanded the XXXI Panzer Corps. He commanded the so-called "Blocking Unit Weidling," and later the LVI Panzer Corps. Named Battle Commander of Berlin in April 1945, on 1 May 1945 Weidling, a recipient of the Knight's Cross with Oak Leaves and Swords, was captured by the Russians. He later died in captivity.

Andrei Andreyevich Vlasov was born in Lomashkino (Novgorod District) on 1 September 1901. After the October Revolution, in 1919 he joined the Red Guard and became an officer. In 1930 he became a member of the Communist Party, and from autumn 1938 served as head of a division headquarters. During the Sino-Japanese War he served as an advisor, and after returning in 1939 assumed command of a division. He was promoted to major-general on

4 June 1940. From January 1941 he commanded the IV Mechanized Corps, which was stationed in the Lvov area in June of that year. In December 1941 as a lieutenant-general he formed the 20th Army and successfully defended Moscow. In 1942 Vlasov was ordered to relieve Leningrad on the Volkhov. During the failed offensive, in July 1942 the commander of the 2nd Shock Army was captured by the Germans near Tukhovechi. As a POW Vlasov was used primarily as a propagandist against Stalin, and at the end of 1944 was named commander-in-chief of the Russian Liberation Army (ROA).

Constantin Voskoboynik took part in the uprising on the Volga in 1921. Under the name Lomashkov he worked as director of the Moscow Office of Weights and Measures. In 1931 his true identity was revealed and he was sent for three years to the Soviet concentration camp in Novosibirsk, where many intellectuals were held. After his release Voskoboynik was initially unemployed, and only with false papers was he able to find work as a teacher in Lokot. He became politically active in autumn 1941 and founded the NSRAP. On 8 January 1942 he was assassinated. Even at the time there were questions as to who was responsible, Soviet partisans or Kaminski.

Appendix 6

Waffen-SS/Army Ranks 1944

SS-Grenadier	Waffen-Grenadier	Grenadier
SS-Sturmmann	Waffen- Sturmmann	Gefreiter
SS-Rottenführer	Waffen-Rottenführer	Obergefreiter
SS-Unterscharführer	Waffen-Unterscharführer	Unteroffizier
SS-Scharführer	Waffen-Scharführer	Unterfeldwebel
SS-Oberscharführer	Waffen- Oberscharführer	Oberfeldwebel
SS-Hauptscharführer	Waffen- Hauptscharführer	Hauptfeldwebel
SS-Untersturmführer	Waffen-Untersturmführer	Leutnant
SS-Obersturmführer	Waffen-Obersturmführer	Oberleutnant
SS-Hauptsturmführer	Waffen-Haupsturmführer	Hauptmann
SS-Sturmbannführer	Waffen-Sturmbannführer	Major
SS-Obersturmbannführer	Waffen-Obersturmbannfuhrer	Oberstleutnant
SS-Standartenführer	Waffen-Standartenführer	Oberst
SS-Oberführer	Waffen-Oberführer	no comparable rank
SS-Brigadeführer	Waffen-Brigadeführer	Generalmajor
SS-Gruppenführer	Waffen-Gruppenführer	Generalleutnant
SS-Obergruppenführer	Waffen-Obergruppenführer	General
SS-Oberstgruppenfuhrer	Waffen-Oberstgruppenführer	Generaloberst

In May 1943 the OKH introduced rank badges for eastern volunteers which were heavily influenced by those worn by the Czarist Army.[70] At the same time rank designations were introduced for native officers.[71] The Russian designations were

2nd lieutenant	podporuchik
1st lieutenant	poruchik
captain	kapitan
major	major
lieutenant-colonel	podpolkovnik
colonel	polkovnik
major-general	Generalmajor

Endnotes

[1] The *SS-Führungshauptamt* used the suffix "*russische Nr. 1 resp. 2*" as a collective term for the eastern Slavic group of Russian peoples made up of (Great) Russians, White Russians (-Ruthenians), and Lesser Russians (Ukrainians).

[2] In Russian: *Narodnaya Strascha "Russkaya Osvoboditelnaya Narodnaya Armiya."*

[3] A Rayon is the smallest Soviet government district and is roughly equivalent to a German *Landkreis* (rural district).

[4] See Appendix 5.

[5] See Appendix 5.

[6] The Soviet command often had known collaborators killed to spread uncertainty and fear among the population of the occupied areas.

[7] See Appendix 5.

[8] See Appendix 5.

[9] See Appendix 5.

[10] See Appendix 5.

[11] Russian Liberation Army

[12] *Oberst* Karl Rübsam had been awarded the German Cross in Gold on 20 March 1942 while serving as commander of the 63rd Rifle Regiment (17th Panzer-Grenadier Brigade).

[13] Report by the Chief of the Security Police and the SD—Detachment Headquarters—12 March 1943: Operations against Bandits in the Area of Einsatzgruppe "B."

[14] SS Battle Group "Zehender" (*SS-Obersturmführer* August Zehender) was formed from elements of the SS Cavalry Division on 16 February 1943, specifically: SS Cavalry Regiment 2, elements of the SS Artillery Regiment, the SS Anti-Tank Battalion, and the SS Flak Battalion, plus a pioneer company, a motor transport column, and the 1st SS Medical Company with the 1st Ambulance Platoon. While the rest of the SS Cavalry Division was in rest positions in the area around Karachev, the battle group was sent to XXXXVII Panzer Corps (*General der Panzertruppen* Lemelsen) in the Orel salient.

[15] See Appendix 5.

[16] Operations Section No. 215/43, secret command matter, dated 13 May 1943.

[17] Special Purpose Division Command 442 had been formed on 18 October 1939 for Korück 580 in Defense District VI with Regional Defense Battalions.

Initially deployed with the 5th Army on the Lower Rhine, in 1942 it was transferred to central Russia. In January and February 1943 the division command was at the disposal of the 4th Army, and in March 1943 the 2nd Panzer Army. The unit was disbanded on 24 August 1944 while part of Army Group Center.

[18] See Appendix 5.

[19] See Appendix 5.

[20] See Appendix 5.

[21] See Appendix 5.

[22] The numbering was not quite correct: the 4th Regiment was completely destroyed in the Sevsk area at the end of August 1943 and was not reformed. So at least on paper the 5th Rifle Regiment was renamed the 4th. As later writings show, however, this was not generally done. For example, the operations order for "Operation Hubertus" still referred to the 5th Regiment.

[23] In February 1945 *Oberstleutnant* Galkin commanded Anti-Tank Brigade R (Russian anti-tank units 10, 11, 13, and 14). Armed with assault rifles and Panzerfaust anti-tank weapons with truck transport, in April 1945 the brigade was readied in the Wotan Position (Altlandsberg – Werneuchen area). Shortly before the big Soviet offensive it was ordered to move to the Friedland area to join the 600th Infantry Division assembled there.

[24] This is the translated Soviet designation. In fact, it was only a tank battalion which had only a few operational vehicles because of shortages of fuel and spare parts. Ultimately the unit was designated a tank company.

[25] As previously related, after the total loss of the 4th Regiment, the 5th Regiment was actually supposed to be designated the 4th Regiment.

[26] See Appendix 5.

[27] The Guards Battalion was made up of particularly reliable and battle-tested soldiers, but in fact it never reached battalion strength. As a rule it was only one or two companies strong.

[28] See: Michaelis, Rolf: *Das SS-Sonderkommando "Dirlewanger,"* Berlin 1999.

[29] See Appendix 5.

[30] See Appendix 5.

[31] See Appendix 5.

[32] See Appendix 5.

[33] See Page 78.

[34] See Appendix 5.

[35] See Page 75.

[36] This is probably an error—it should probably read League of German Maidens girls.

[37] See Appendix 5.

[38] See Appendix 5.

[39] See Appendix 5.

[40] See Appendix 5.

[41] The General Commissariat of "White Ruthenia" was initially part of the Reich Commissariat "Ostland," in which the Senior SS and Police Commander "B"—renamed Senior SS and Police Commander "Northern Russia and Ostland in 1942—was responsible for security. This initially assigned an SS and police commander to each of the four general commissariats: Estonia, Latvia, Lithuania, and White Ruthenia. On 1 October 1942 the troops of the commander of the Order Police in Minsk under the Senior SS and Police Commander "White Ruthenia" numbered 1,394 Germans and 9,830 non-Germans. Of the latter, 1,456 men were assigned to the White Ruthenian Police Battalions 46-49.

[42] They were: the "Anhalt" Brigade, which was deployed as part of the 14th Infantry Division (VI Army Corps) in the area south and southeast of Grayevo. It consisted of SS Police Regiment 2 (established on 12 July 1944 from the remnants of SS Police Regiments 2, 22, 24, 26, and Police Rifle Regiments 34 and 36) and SS Police Regiment 4. SS Police Regiment 17, which was attached to the "Brauer" Division (left neighbor of the "Anhalt" Brigade) and deployed in the front line in the area south and southeast of Raygrod.

[43] SS-FHA Amt II Org.Abt. Ia/II, diary No. 2590/44 secret command matter of 18 August 1944.

[44] The same can be said of the 11th SS Volunteer Panzer-Grenadier Division "Nordland." Only about 15% of the men serving in the two SS Panzer-Grenadier Regiments 23 "Norge" and 24 "Danmark" were Norwegians and Danes. The rest were ethnic Germans from Rumania, See: Michaelis, Rolf: *The 11. SS-Freiwilligen-Panzer-Grenadier-Division "Nordland,"* Schiffer Publishing 2008.

[45] See Page 62.

[46] In the police units there were no ranks comparable to Wachtmeister and Meister.

[47] The German offices were wrong in this. As doubts existed as to the reliability of the former policemen, no units of the *30. Waffen-Grenadier-Division der SS (russische Nr. 2)* were employed in the suppression of the Warsaw uprising.

[48] De facto they were not Polish uniforms but Schutzmannschaft (police) uniforms.

[49] Among these were those whose loyalty was uncertain. Because of time constraints, however, the division command was unable to sort out all the unreliable men during the transfer west.

[50] Partisans were designated bandits in eastern and southern Europe and terrorists in western and northwestern Europe.

[51] Commander-in-Chief West, war diary Ia No. 7188/44 secret command matter.

[52] It is not surprising that the terrorists' movement grew steadily given the support they received from England and America. Areas of resistance in summer 1944 were the Ardennes and in the Henne District, in Brittany, the High Alps, and the Limoges area. On 2 June 1944 600 French rebels appeared en masse for the first time in Figeac (120 km NE of Toulouse). The so-called "*Armée secrete*" began with mobilization in the liberated areas and was equipped with heavy weapons.

[53] Commander-in-Chief West, war diary Ia No. 7259/44 secret command matter.

[54] Commander-in-Chief West, war diary Ia No. 7378/44 secret command matter.

[55] Commander-in-Chief West, war diary Ia No. 7439/44 secret command matter.

[56] After responsibility for the immediate securing and defense of the west position and the *Westwall* was transferred to Himmler on 1 September 1944, he at once ordered the restoration of the defense installations partly disassembled in the previous years. 200,000 workers were mobilized within a few days, including the approximately 2,400 foreigners formerly members of the *30. Waffen-Grenadier-Division der SS (russische Nr. 2)*.

[57] The so-called "Muravyev" Battalion was formed on 12 September 1944 from 3 officers and 88 men of the 1st Regiment and 6 officers and 754 men of the 2nd Regiment, plus 2 officers and 37 men of the Reconnaissance Battalion.

[58] Regimental commander: *SS-Hauptsturmführer und Hauptmann der Schutzpolizei* Schmidt.

[59] Ost-Bataillon 654 was formed on 23 October 1944 in the area west of Staraya Russa from the Russian Security Battalion 510 established in the summer and transferred to the Chaumont area (France). The battalion was ordered disbanded on 17 February 1945 and the Russian members were assigned to the 600th Infantry Division (Russian). It was the only army unit attached to the SS unit.

[60] High Command Army Group G, Chief-of-Staff Ia diary No. 3854/44 secret command matter of 18/11/44.

[61] Chief of Staff Commander-in-Chief West, Ia diary No. 19675/44 secret command matter of 19 November 1944.

[62] Wounded German soldiers had previously crossed into Switzerland through a hole in the border fence.

[63] SS-FHA, diary No. 164/45 secret command matter.

[64] See: Michaelis, Rolf: *Die Grenadier-Divisionen der Waffen-SS Teil III*, Erlangen 1995.

[65] The Russian word "drushina" means battle group. The designation thus refers to the original employment of the men, who were to be employed in small-scale diversionary actions.

[66] The unit envisaged for this purpose, Kampfgeschwader 200, an experimental unit under the Commander-in-Chief of the Luftwaffe, was incapable of such operations because of fuel shortages.

[67] *SS-Oberführer* Naumann had been commander of SD Einsatzgruppe "B" from 1941 to March 1942.

[68] In mid-April 1944 the 1st Anti-Fascist Brigade was surrounded by German troops in the area of the Zaybki railway station during "Operation Spring Festival." Approximately 300 former members of the SS Unit "Drushina" were killed in the fighting or captured. Radionov was among the fallen.

[69] See Appendix 5.

[70] Decree by the OKH/Gen.St.d.H./Gen.Qu./IVa (III, 3) Az. 985 d, No. I/14124/ of 29 May 1943.

[71] Decree by the OKH/Gen.St.d.H./Gen. d. Osttruppen, No. 1200/43 of 9 May 1943.

Register of Names

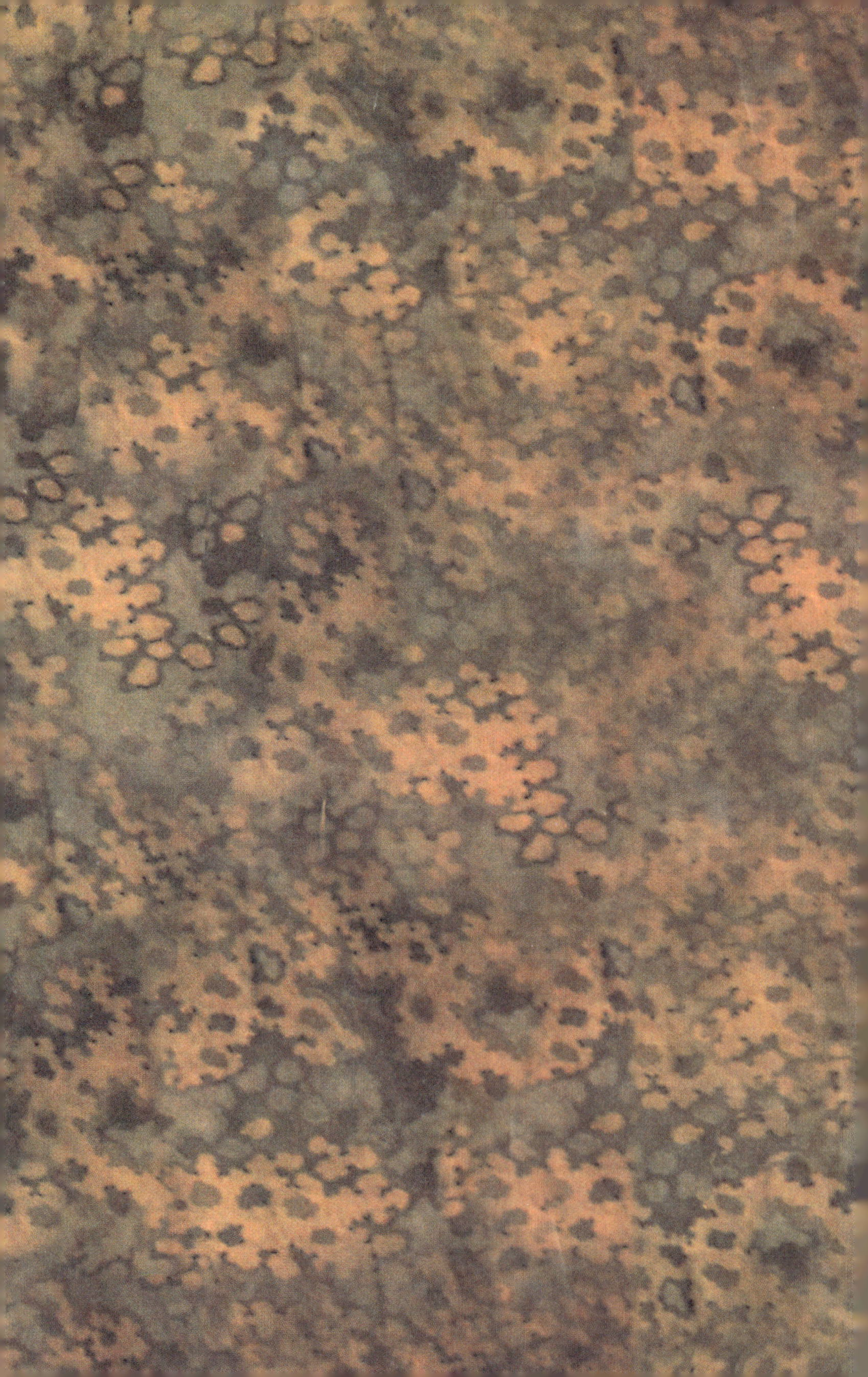